BEING FRANK

BEING FRANK

The Frank Houston Story

Hazel Houston

Marshall Pickering

Marshall Morgan and Scott
Marshall Pickering
34–42 Cleveland Street, London, W1P 5FB U.K.

First published in 1989 by Marshall Morgan and Scott Publications
Ltd. Part of the Marshall Pickering Holdings Group

Scripture quotations are from the King James Version.

British Library Cataloguing in Publication Data
Houston, Hazel
  Being Frank.
  1. Christian church, Evangelicism.
  Houston, Frank
  I. Title
  277.3'0092'4

ISBN: 0 551 01886 0

Text Set in Baskerville by Prima Graphics, Camberley, Surrey
Printed in Great Britain by Collins, Glasgow

Acknowledgments

I want to thank all who have made a contribution to this book.

My husband. Without him there would be no story. I appreciate the help he gave me (when I could nail him down to get his help.)

Our children, Maureen, Graeme, Brian, Beverley and Judith, who not only gave their father to the ministry but have helped me by their interest in the project and their willingness to jog my memory when it was time to write about them.

Colin Whittaker who pressured me into action frequently, saying, 'Get it all down Hazel,' and for his Foreword.

Jean Mullins, who took the time to read and correct the manuscript, and Robert Ferguson, who put aside his scriptural study of the anointing to correct the story of one of God's anointed.

The story is true but, in consideration for the feelings of the living and in respect for the dead, some names have been changed.

Contents

Foreword

Over a good number of years I had heard the name of Frank Houston mentioned with increasing frequency in connection with the Revival in New Zealand. Next news his name was linked with an amazing story concerning the planting of a new church in Sydney, Australia. I just hoped that one day I would have an opportunity to meet this person who was so obviously an outstanding servant of the Lord with a tremendous ministry of faith and power.

Some of the stories about him which filtered through to my editorial desk, when I was the editor of *Redemption Tidings*, were in the Smith Wigglesworth category. I knew that he had served as the General Superintendent of Assemblies of God in New Zealand and that he had built up a flourishing church there as well as conducting numerous successful evangelistic and healing crusades. Whenever the move of God in New Zealand in the early 1970s was mentioned, his name always seemed to crop up somewhere.

It was in the late 1970s that news began to reach us that this chap Houston had done the crack-pot thing of leaving his flourishing church in New Zealand to pioneer a new church in Sydney. It all sounded quite crazy. We rather gathered that 'the Aussies' were not exactly thrilled about being invaded by 'this upstart Houston from little old New Zealand.' After all, he was fifty-five years old and should have known better. We gathered that he had less than a dozen people in his congregation when he started but he had hired a room in one of the big hotels in Sydney and was 'really going for it'. We waited for the inevitable crash – but it never happened. Instead we began to hear of God doing great things in Frank Houston's meetings, with big crowds flocking to them. Within eight years he had built up a congregation of around two thousand in one of the roughest areas in one of the toughest cities Down Under. Not content with that, he had also planted fourteen other new churches around New South Wales. As a result the Aussies had taken him to their hearts and had voted him onto the Assemblies of God Executive Council.

In 1985 Frank Houston was invited to be one of the guest speakers at the Assemblies of God Minehead Celebration and I was afforded the long awaited pleasure of meeting him. My wife and I shared a table in the dining room with Frank and his wife Hazel throughout the week and it was the beginning of a warm friendship. I interviewed him in my capacity as editor and was able to ask him a lot of searching questions. As conference vice-chairman I was kept in close proximity with him throughout the week and had the opportunity of observing him carefully as he preached, lectured and ministered to the sick. The more I saw of him and the more I heard him, the more my heart warmed to him. He has a delightful sense of humour and is a born communicator. We saw miracles happen that week as he ministered in successive meetings. The level of faith in the thousands present was raised in every meeting. Yet there was no pride or pretentiousness. His ministry was Christ-exalting, God-glorifying, and people-blessing. In spite of the success God has given to him, Frank Houston remains delightfully natural and unspoiled. In 1987 my wife and I had theprivilege of ministering in their church in Sydney, Australia, and witnessing the work first hand. We had the additional benefit of staying with them in their home and seeing them away from the public eye. I was not disappointed; in Frank Houston

I observed a totally acceptable face of power-evangelism.

The saying has been repeated almost *ad nauseum* that 'God's methods are men', but frequently that is only a half-truth. The whole truth in this particular case is certainly: 'God's methods are men and women.' Frank and Hazel Houston are as inseparable a team as were Aquilla and Priscilla, or Zacharias and Elisabeth. They blend together perfectly and yet they are as difficult as chalk and cheese. Hazel is strong – physically, mentally, and spiritually – and she has needed all these attributes down through the years as she has been called to cope with more than her share of crises. Frank is less robust; physically and mentally he has been brought to breaking point more than once. Yet one feels this vulnerability is the very thing which has given him a sensitivity to suffering to which people relate and warm.

This is a story full of human interest. Frank and Hazel Houston have suffered and paid a price for the ministry which they are exercising so successfully today. They both started out as officers in the Salvation Army. Their roots, spiritual and natural, are exposed here for all to see. This book will make you cry as well as laugh. It will set you praying harder as well as praising more. Hazel Houston is the only one who could have written this story in its fullness. She has done it well and in doing so has placed the church at large in her debt. This book will increase your faith. All who are now entering into what Peter Wagner calls 'The Third Wave', with a strong desire to see the supernatural restored to the Church, will be helped by this book. And those Pentecostals and Charismatics who are in danger of settling down into a comfy, cosy, non-supernatural, respectable evangelicalism, will be suitably rebuked and challenged 'to rekindle the flame'.

Colin Whittaker
Pastor of The Mount of Olives,
Bristol
January 1989

Chapter 1

THE END OF THE BEGINNING

It was ten o'clock in the morning when Frank disappeared. For three weeks I had watched him being smothered by depression. His eyes were strained and his concentration poor.

'Feel this lump in my neck,' he would say to me. I could never feel a lump but he would get angry when I told him so. Fearing another nervous breakdown, I talked to our doctor. He listened to my story but he didn't seem to realise the seriousness of it. If only Frank had come with me, but he wouldn't. He would be very angry if he had known I was there.

'I don't think he'll have a breakdown. He simply needs a holiday. Take him to the mountains.'

'What! On a Salvation Army officer's salary? Impossible.' Our salary of six pounds a week didn't stretch to luxuries even in 1954.

The crash happened on the day the Salvation Army Divisional Commander was due to audit the books. Frank and I had worked on them together for an hour finalising details in preparation. I should have been prepared for what happened as I had noticed moments when he would stare blankly into space.

Then he would continue working. When all was finished he drove to the Post Office to get some stamps or so he said. When he wasn't back by ten o'clock I began to worry. Colonel Bethe arrived sharp at ten thirty. Still Frank was not back. Something had to be wrong for he was never late for appointments.

'Frank has gone to post some letters. He should be

back at any moment,' I explained. Colonel Bethe seemed quite unconcerned.

While he settled himself in the lounge with the ledgers and record books, I became an agitated clock watcher, pacing to the gate and back every ten minutes. No sign of Frank. I checked our two small boys playing happily in the spring sunshine and fed our three-week-old baby girl. This kept me from total panic.

As the morning wore on my anxiety became unbearable. I felt I had to share it with someone. I would tell Colonel Bethe. He might be able to tell me what to do. He didn't seem very happy at my interruption.

'Colonel, Frank still isn't back. He's been gone for two hours. What shall I do?'

'Don't worry. I'm sure he'll be back soon.' How could he sit there and say that. To me it seemed impossible that anyone could remain unconcerned when I was in such a turmoil.

'I think I'll tell the police. They might look for him.'

'A person has to be gone for more than two hours before the police will regard him as missing.' He was right.

Worse was to come. Lunchtime was over and Brian, still only eighteen months old, went down for his afternoon sleep while Graeme went back to the garden to play. Thank God my tension was not affecting them. I tried to concentrate on household chores but the feeling of impending disaster which gripped me made it very difficult.

Pray, I must pray. God will bring Frank back. Many times we had preached on prayer. Now I must put it into practice.

'God, keep him safe and bring him home.' It seemed God wasn't listening. I still had no peace and Frank didn't return.

Suddenly Colonel Bethe appeared with some books in his hand. He dropped a bombshell when he said,

'There appears to be a discrepancy in the books. They don't balance with each other. Can you explain this?' My stomach knotted in disbelief.

'No I cannot explain it.' I had no idea what had happened. This was an area of church life in which I had no part. I left it entirely to Frank and the church treasurer.

'This could be a police matter you know.'

I looked at him in shocked silence. How could he say that before he talked with Frank or the treasurer.

Although I didn't ask him how much the books were out and he didn't tell me, I knew we were not thieves. Had this man no compassion nor trust in officers who had served in the Army for twelve years? I was glad to see him turn his shiny shoes in the direction of the lounge. All respect I had for him faded at that moment.

Mid-afternoon, Maureen, our six-year-old daughter, rushed in from school full of the events of the day. It was hard to stay still long enough to listen to her eager chatter, but that restored some calm to my spirit. I guessed now why Frank hadn't come home but that still did not tell me where he was.

I felt totally alone now. To whom could I go? Salvation Army officers were advised not to make friends in the congregation and after the events of the day I could not go to Colonel Bethe. The afternoon dragged on. I prayed again, 'Lord give me strength to meet whatever comes. Help me to face the church board when they come for the meeting tonight.'

I knew it could only be by divine grace that I could face those men, especially the one we called the 'whistling man'. As well as being a board member he was Sunday School superintendent and a bandsman. He earned his nickname by always whistling when the band marched into services. He knew it would annoy the Captain.

Maybe if I left the door open the men would walk

in without bothering me. Colonel Bethe could explain Frank's absence in whichever way he chose. The children demanded my attention.

'Mummy, read me the Peter Rabbit book.'

'No, we had that one last night. I want the one about Noah and the Ark.'

'Come on all of you. It's time for bed.' As I undressed them and listened to their prayers I heard the various members of the board arrive. I was right when I thought they would just walk in. I had avoided the embarrassment of meeting them. Perhaps it would have been better if I had seen them for most were kindly men. Now there was nothing to occupy my thoughts except the problems of the moment. If there had been a car accident I'd have heard by now.

'God, why can't I trust you? Why can't I pray?' There seemed no answers. Instead doubts and queries flooded my mind. What would our future hold? Could we go on being Salvation Army officers? Frank had been increasingly frustrated in his work and often talked about resigning. Sometimes we failed to send in the required weekly reports. In the next mail there would be a letter demanding an explanation.

Dear Captain,
We have not received your visitation report for this week. Please tell us how many hours' visitation you have done and how many people you have prayed with. We need this information immediately.
God bless you,
Yours faithfully,
Henry Bethe.
Colonel.

Maybe we had visited an officer in another town without asking permission. The rules and regulations said we had to ask headquarters before leaving our area but the book contained so many rules that we never mastered them all. None of that mattered now.

The present was more important than all that had happened in the past and my only worry was where Frank might be.

It would have been easier to go looking for him than helplessly waiting. It didn't occur to me until then that Frank had taken the car and could be miles away by now. I decided to wait another half hour and then phone the police, no matter what anyone else said.

The door bell interrupted my reverie. Frank was home. I knew it. But I didn't want to open the door for fear of what I might find. One look told me everything. He stared vacantly at me as he leaned on the two men who had brought him home. The truth hit me hard. Frank was an emotional and mental wreck.

The two men, members of the church, helped me get him into bed. There was no sign of recognition – hysterical amnesia the doctors called it.

'He wandered into our place about an hour ago. We could see he was ill,' the men said.

'The car. Where is the car? Was he driving it?'

'He was but we have driven it here.'

How could anyone drive a car in that condition? I realised that the board would have to be told about Frank's state, but not yet. This was something I must handle myself. If the 'whistling man' saw him it would be all over town in no time. I could imagine him saying that the Army Captain was out of his mind. It was a horrifying thought. No, I couldn't tell them now.

I was uneasy at the way Frank tossed from side to side flinging his arms wildly in every direction. Would he sleep through the night or would he wander off again in his confusion? Whatever he did there was no way I would sleep easy with that uncertainty on my mind. Sleeping pills – I must get some sleeping pills. If I was sure he was sleeping I would sleep. I phoned the doctor.

'Doctor, Frank has had a breakdown. No, there is no need to come tonight. If you could prescribe some sleeping pills that will be enough.'

'I'll send round some capsules. Give him two and I will call in the morning.'

Almost as soon as the capsules slipped down Frank's throat the restlessness ceased while the stress of the last few hours drained away. To avoid any fuss I determined to tell the Colonel as he was about to leave but I'm sure he knew that Frank was home.

'I'd like to see the Captain before I go,' he said when I told him.

'He's already asleep and I don't want him disturbed.'

Thankfully that was the truth for I was convinced it would not be in our best interests for Colonel Bethe to see Frank just then. His accusations still rankled in my mind. He stalked off down the path, his displeasure showing in his face. After shutting the door, hiding the car keys and checking on the children, I fell into bed glad that a nightmare day was over.

'Lord watch over us and give us a better day tomorrow!' It was a prayer of desperate hope rather than solid faith. God seemed well and truly hidden beneath the events of this unforgettable day.

With morning came new strength. Rested in mind and body I felt prepared to face whatever the day might bring. Frank was still asleep when the children came tumbling out for breakfast. Suddenly the sound of singing came floating down to the kitchen. For the first time in twenty-four hours I laughed.

Fancy the Salvation Army Captain singing Grace Kelly's song from the film *High Society*. 'True Love' seemed to be a favourite tune.

It was a proper recital for he sang it over and over in a voice not yet spoiled by preaching. He might have sung a hymn or chorus. Did his singing foretell a brighter day? It was not to be. As the sedative wore off his depression returned. The only difference between that and the next three mornings was the song he sang and the huge congregation he imagined had come to hear his preaching.

'Hazel,' he'd say. 'Here are all these people waiting for the meeting to begin and we have no pianist. Will you get one?' I humoured him by saying I would. These were the only bright spots in the day.

On the fourth morning he asked me to take him to the hospital. He didn't need to ask twice. After a quick call to warn them we were coming, I piled the children into the car, got Frank aboard and we were off before he could change his mind.

The hospital was an old stone building with a forbidding atmosphere – enough to discourage anyone who was already depressed. Frank hesitated at the door. I couldn't let him change his mind now.

'Come on dear, the doctor will be waiting for you.' The doctor was waiting. His questions were few. Dr West understood the situation perfectly. He seemed to sum up the problem from Frank's sagging shoulders and downcast eyes.

'I think you had better stay with us for a few days.'

'I need to go home to get my razor and toilet gear.'

Frantically I told the doctor, by signs from behind Frank's back, that he wouldn't return. Dr West did some more coaxing. Frank hesitated and then agreed to stay. I could see a look of relief on his face as he walked away with the doctor. He straightened himself and walked more surely than he had since the day he disappeared. He said later it was as though a load had rolled off his shoulders at that moment. He felt secure. He may have felt secure but there was nothing but insecurity for me. And questions.

'Why God? Why have you allowed this to happen again?' There had been an earlier breakdown and I'd prayed that there would never be another. Didn't God know that I felt I couldn't cope with a sick husband and four children, the youngest only three weeks old.

'Why, God, why? why why?' Heaven wasn't answering. Instead of the burden lifting, such a blackness smothered my soul that I didn't seem able to reach God. My prayers were not getting beyond the ceiling, I thought. In reality, my understanding and knowledge of evil forces was nil. Up to this time spiritual warfare had consisted of a battle over the rights and wrongs of ballroom dancing or the movies and I hadn't worried about those since the first year I was born of the Spirit of God. Far into the night I wrestled with these powers of darkness. Sleep eluded me and, except for the baby's cry for a midnight feed, the silent hours dragged on undisturbed.

At four in the morning, tired and depressed myself, I knew that I could not battle this thing alone. God was my helper: the Bible said so.

'God, you know all about the whys, I don't. I give it all to you.' Inexplicable light flooded the room and I fell asleep to awaken three hours later renewed and at peace. I wondered why I had taken so long to really yield to God in this way. What lessons He was beginning to teach me. But He knew what battles were still ahead and the lessons of faith which I needed to know if I was to win through to the place He had for me – for us. When I went to the grocery store that day it suddenly occurred to me that what little money I possessed would have to last a long time. Our salary would cease at the end of the week. Sure, government assistance was available, but from the time I lodged an application until the money actually arrived was likely to be weeks. The Social Welfare Department was never in a hurry.

Again I thought over our position as Salvation Army officers. The Salvation Army had been our life for years. We had found the Lord through its ministry and the call to be officers in its ranks was very real. If we were to leave we would need to be just as sure it was God bringing us out. I shook my head

Why was I thinking like this? Frank had only just entered hospital.

Common sense said wait until you know the doctor's report and what the Salvation Army leaders have to say about it.

I'm sure little promptings of the Spirit were beginning to awaken me to the voice of God. The feeling that our work as officers was finished became stronger until I was certain that life would take a new direction. I never thought that we would have to give up being Salvationists, but a number of questions rushed to my mind. Where would we live? What could Frank do after so long away from the secular workforce?

Houses for rent were hard to find. The one we were living in was owned by the Salvation Army and made available furnished to the officer in charge of the Corps. They'd need it now for our replacement. We would have to move out soon.

We all began to look forward to our visits to daddy in the hospital. We'd sit in the garden and he would tell us about his life there. After a complete physical examination Dr West confirmed there really was no lump in Frank's neck as he claimed there was. He explained that nervous breakdowns were often accompanied by physical symptoms which had no physical cause. After this Frank began to improve rapidly. The effects of the insulin treatment amused him.

'Today I saw two of Dr West as he came round the ward,' he told us. 'When I talked to him it was difficult to tell which one was real!'

Another time he had such a violent reaction to the drug he went dancing down the ward. 'The nurses grabbed me, flung me on the bed and poured heaps of glucose down my throat to counter the effects of the insulin' he laughed. It was wonderful to see his old sense of humour returning.

Encouraged by the doctor, he eventually recalled the events of the day he disappeared. He had posted his letters and then driven miles through the city and up a winding road to the top of a hill. It didn't seem possible that he had driven all that way without an accident. He recalled a stranger asking if he was ill and suggesting he bring him home, but Frank resisted that suggestion. What took him to the home of those church people? We were both sure it was the hand of God that led him.

The day came when I was able to talk to him about the 'missing' money. It was as I had guessed. He had shown amounts he had not collected, always hoping he could do it tomorrow. He was never well enough.

The root of the problem was the fear of failure and the probability that he would be appointed to a smaller church if he had not reached the target set by headquarters for that appeal.

Our major problem during those days was that of money. I had to feed the children somehow, which was no easy matter when we had no income. The grocer at the end of the street allowed me to charge groceries to an account.

At least the grocer trusted me. Twice Colonel Bethe phoned to see if I had received any benefit from the Social Welfare. Once he gave me five pounds ($10) and the offer of getting clothes from the Samaritan Department. I cringed at the thought. Over the years I had sorted clothes which had been sent to the Army. Some of them were so dirty and in poor repair I shuddered at the thought of them. We would manage somehow.

At last a senior officer from Territorial Headquarters came to talk to me. 'Have you thought about your future?' he asked.

'A little, but I have not discussed it with Frank. I am beginning to think we should resign from officership.'

'You don't need to do that but we will have to take you out of church work and put you in social work. We have an appointment for you working with homeless men.'

'Frank would never do that kind of work. He has been

called to preach.' The officer looked strangely at me.

'Don't you realise that Frank will never preach again.' I was dumbfounded. In a flash I saw discoveries I had unconsciously made as I had been seeking God. His call had not changed nor could miracles of earlier years be forgotten. I knew I'd heard a lie from hell.

'He will preach again.' I was shouting. How could the man say that. His understanding of the situation and mine were totally different.

It was a week after Frank's discharge from hospital that we received a telegram asking Frank to contact the Divisional Headquarters. What now I thought. When Frank went to see him, Colonel Bethe came straight to the point.

'Someone has been collecting with an official collecting book in the district. Was it your wife?' Frank walked out of the office without answering. He could scarcely tell me of the accusation. 'What do they think I am?' I shouted angrily. 'Whoever it was collecting it wasn't me.'

The pressure was really on now. Once more we had experienced the hurt of not being trusted. It was impossible to justify ourselves but the Spirit reminded us that it is God who justifies and years later we were to experience that justification when officers who were sick and discouraged came to us for prayer and help. Now, certain as we were that God had called us into the Army, we were certain He was calling us out.

Sadly we posted our resignation not only from the ministry but from the Army which we loved. Nothing more was said about the accusations and we were convinced that they knew we were innocent. The call continued but it would be in a different direction. Now we were without home or job. All we possessed were six forks, two pairs of blankets, and an old radio. With four children to provide for, God was going to have to do some miracles and do them quickly. But then Frank's life had begun with a miracle.

Chapter 2

THE IRISH FACTOR

The twenty-second of April 1922 had been a busy day
for Frank and Annie Houston. Their oldest child was
six and Annie had managed to create a special dinner
in spite of the shortage of finance and her very
pregnant condition. She was clearing away the remains
of the meal when the contractions began at five-minute
intervals.

'Frank, I think it's time to get Arthur Tucknott to
take me to Nurse Jackman's. The baby's coming.'

Gretha Rebecca danced round excitedly. The baby
was coming on her birthday. Linda was only two and
didn't care. Their father grabbed his old beret off its
hook and hurried out to his bicycle. Furiously he
pedalled the three blocks to the Tucknott residence.

'Hurry Arthur, get your truck out. Annie's about to
have the baby,' he gasped in his rich Irish brogue.
Arthur Tucknott owned one of the few vehicles
around in 1922.

'Leave your bike here, Frank. You can get it later,'
he said as he cranked the truck into life.

Annie was waiting for them bag in hand. They sat
her between them on the very hard seat of the smart
blue truck. Arthur released the hand brake and pushed
the lever on the steering column to set it in motion.
The solid-tyred vehicle seemed to hit every pothole in
the unsealed road.

'Hurry,' she gasped as another contraction gripped
her.

'He's doing thirty miles an hour now and he can't

go any faster,' Frank rebuked her. 'It will be better when we get on the tarseal.'

Annie was relieved when they pulled up at the midwife's house fifteen minutes later. Frank hurried her along the path anxious to get her into the midwife's care. He gave her a quick kiss goodbye and beat a hasty retreat encouraged by Nurse Jackman. Childbirth was women's business in those days. Fathers were a nuisance and must go home to wait. Annie didn't mind. She didn't expect any complications with the birth. Her other two children were born without any problems.

'Come along dear,' said Nurse Jackman thickly, as she picked up Annie's bag. Her speech was slurred.

'This woman's drunk,' Annie thought but there was nothing she could do about the situation now. The baby's arrival was too close. The impending birth blotted out the implications of the whiskey bottle sitting on a nearby table. Annie prayed that God would be with her, over-ruling the situation.

It wasn't too long before the lusty crying of the baby boy filled the room. Nurse Jackman laid him in a cot while she attended to the mother between gulps at the whiskey bottle. A chilled baby was bathed an hour later.

Days of neglect followed as the midwife tried to cope with mother, baby and whiskey bottle. Even Frank's Irish anger made no difference. Three weeks later the baby was admitted to hospital, his small frame wracked with pneumonia.

Frank and Annie watched his struggle for life as the often fatal disease advanced to crisis point. There were no antibiotics. He was given the best medication possible and the help of a steam tent but it wasn't enough. Complications set in. Meningitis, the doctor thought. Frank and Annie were called to the hospital.

'Come quickly. We think your baby is dying,' the voice said. Frank was shocked. This will destroy

Annie, he thought. All the way to the hospital he held her hand trying to console her, but the tears kept on falling. As they walked the endless length of corridor leading to the ward they wondered if God would really let their baby die. The local Anglican vicar happened to be visiting the hospital. When he saw their distress he stopped to ask the reason, offering his help although he knew they were not Anglicans. The Rev Weller was a man of great compassion.

'Whatever is wrong? Can I be of any help?'

'Rev Weller, our baby is dying. They do not think he will last the day,' Frank told him, his strong body shaken by deeps sobs.

'Would you like me to baptise him and pray for him?' the minister asked.

Now the Houstons were Baptists. At least Annie was. Frank wasn't given to going to church although he believed in God. Anyway in a time like this denomination didn't matter.

'Would you really do that? We would be so grateful,' Frank assured him.

Together they walked to the ward where the baby still clung to life.

'What is the baby's name,' Rev Weller asked.

'William Francis.' The vicar asked the nurse for some water and in a simple ceremony he sprinkled the baby's head.

'I baptise you William Francis Houston in the name of the Father, Son and Holy Spirit,' he intoned. Putting aside the water he reached into the steam tent placing his hand gently on the frail body. 'Lord Jesus, I ask you to heal this baby by your divine power. Amen.' This man of faith assured Frank and Annie that he believed the baby would recover. 'God answers prayer,' he encouraged.

It was hard to cling to that assurance as they watched their tiny son gasping for breath. A miracle had already begun, for God's hand was upon this child though they could not see it then. His was an interesting heritage. His mother, of German–English descent, had suffered much in her life.

Her mother had died when she was born and she had been reared by a succession of stepmothers. There would be five in all but only the first three were to have much influence on her life. One made her sit at the kitchen bench for her meals while the rest of the family ate in the dining room. She was beaten often.

Annie did not sorrow when that stepmother died. In spite of hurts and insecurities she carried no bitterness. Her faith in God enabled her to keep a sense of humour which helped her keep a forgiving spirit, for Annie Houston never said a bad word about anybody. She'd developed a sense of humour which endeared her to her four children.

Frank Houston had emigrated from Ireland when he was twenty. He had already become a staunch Orangeman and brought with him a dislike of Roman Catholics. In his line were many clergy including bishops who over centuries had served in the Church of England. This was the heritage of William Francis, who should have been Francis William.

For some reason known only to himself, Frank registered his children with the name they would use as their second name. A little Irish perverseness some said. By the time Frank junior was seven, the Great Depression had hit New Zealand.

Money was scarcer than ever but his father was never out of work. While many of their friends lost their homes the Houstons managed to keep the house they were buying. It was a house which hid a mixture of experiences.

There were tempestuous times when young Frank was terrorised by his father's fits of Irish temper. Often it seemed uncontrollable. Frank never forgot the day his father banged his head on the old meat safe hanging outside the kitchen door. Filled with pain

27

and anger, he grabbed the axe and smashed the safe into a heap of rubble.

Another time when Gretha displeased him by not cleaning out the canary cage he threw it at her. The children would scuttle to the safe places they had discovered. There were times when father would go outside, look around, then announce, 'There will be an earthquake tonight.' It was small comfort to the children who knew he was often right in his predictions. They had horrible memories of the night when the house rocked violently, shaking them out of sleep. Bottles crashed out of cupboards and bricks were thrown out of the chimney onto the beds of two terrified girls. As their father tried to walk along the passage to rescue them he was thrown from one side to the other. He gathered the children in the doorway till the rocking had subsided.

The electricity failed, plunging the neighbourhood into darkness, but the Houston's gas lights were still burning. Fear changed to giggles when all the neighbours' children climbed into one bed. There was comfort in company of others but they always feared earthquakes and their father's uncanny predictions.

They loved the evenings when the events of the day slipped into the past and they sat round their father to hear their favourite stories of his long trip on the boat from Ireland and the storms he experienced at sea.

'The waves were thirty feet high and the boat would go up and over them, throwing people round or making them so sick they had to stay in bed.' The children sat spellbound as their father became the hero in this dramatic scene. Another favourite was that of the Giants Causeway he'd left behind in Ireland. The rocks became Giant's foot prints and Irish Leprechauns hid in the cracks.

The story would change to one from the Bible. These were usually of the type which told of the judgement of God.

'God told Noah to take the animals into the ark because He would send a big flood. The people were so wicked. It rained and rained till the water was so deep all the people except Noah and his family were drowned,' he told them. 'You kids had better be good for God is watching you.'

Four small children quaked at the thought of God glaring down from the dizzy heights of heaven waiting to pounce on them. Then they'd imagine the trumpets sounding to herald the second coming of Jesus as father graphically described the scene. This became an event to be feared rather than welcomed. Annie's teaching was of a gentler kind. She taught the children to pray.

Every Sunday morning she walked them three miles to church and home again. Back they went for afternoon Sunday School and the third time in the day they walked back for the evening service. Sunday was God's day. No shoes to be cleaned or sports to be played. Church was an experience they all enjoyed although there was the occasional unspiritual event Annie had trouble controlling.

'See that woman's hat,' Frank said, nudging Allan in the ribs. 'She's still got the price tag hanging on it.' As that prim and devout soul nodded her head in prayer the price tag flipped up and down. The children started to giggle. Annie tried to reprimand them for their frivolous behaviour but when she glimpsed the tag announcing to all that the hat cost £2 she joined their amusement.

How they wished their father would come to church with them, but he rarely did. He had been hurt when a denomination refused to baptise him. He would never tell us why. Sometimes he would go at Christmas. That was a special time. Every evening for months beforehand father would lock himself in his shed. The children were filled with curiosity. What could he be doing? He couldn't be mending shoes. He'd done that

29

last week. Somehow every Christmas there were toys in their stockings, fashioned from bits and pieces found in that shed. The greatest delight was getting fourteen pennies to spend however they pleased.

The first Christmas after Gretha started work her employer gave her a bottle of parsnip wine. Now Annie, who had signed the pledge when she was a girl, had no idea how potent parsnip wine could be. She poured herself a glass of what she thought was soft drink and then a second. Next thing she came waltzing out to her children waving her arms in front of her.

'I'm floating, I'm floating,' she declared just as a salesman came to the door. The children were horrified. Their mother – tipsy. Then they began to laugh. They vowed never to tell their father. There were some secrets that father must never know because of his wrath. But he could also laugh when it suited him. The day Annie emptied the teapot out the back door and caught the butcher full in the face with tea leaves intended for the garden he laughed louder than them all.

Tea leaves must have been good for the garden for there were always an abundance of flowers in the front of the house and rows of fresh vegetables at the back. Frank and Allan were responsible to help with the weeding and hoeing.

Frank had a habit of reducing the parsnips by an alarming number for he hated eating them. As an adult he would often declare that man was not structured for eating parsnips.

If the weeding was not done properly there would be trouble.

'Hey, ye young varmints, ye haven't done it properly. Ye'll get no tea till ye have,' father would yell. Back the boys would go, each blaming the other for the unfinished task. On most of these occasions Frank would win the ensuing battle but the tables turned when Allan grew taller. Frank found it humiliating to be older yet getting beaten. Often when father and son were working in the garden together they'd hear Mr Burke, the Catholic neighbour, working in his. Now Frank senior, being a staunch Orangeman, said to Frank junior, 'Frank walk down by the fence and shout "To hell with the Pope."' Obediently the small boy would do it.

'To hell with the Pope, to hell with the Pope,' he'd chant. Young Frank developed a dislike for Catholics as he said it. For a time Mr Burke would move to the other side of his garden without saying a word. Finally he decided the best course of action was to beat them at their own game. When he heard young Frank on the other side of the fence he'd get in first with the 'to hell with the Pope' bit, thus defusing the situation.

The Catholic and Protestant children engaged in wordy battles on the way to their respective schools.

'Cattle dogs, cattle dogs,' the Protestants cried derisively, young Frank shouting louder than the rest.

He wasn't the son of an Orangeman for nothing.

'Prody dogs, prody dogs,' the Catholics called back determined not to be outdone.

'To hell with the Pope.' Frank would fling the final insult. What would Mr Burke and his father have said had they known that Frank would be invited to meet Pope John Paul the second when he visited Australia in 1987!

School days were not the easiest for Frank. He was so excited the first day, instantly falling in love with his teacher. Miss Pitcher was kind and understanding but Frank was shocked when his friend, Finn, was made to stand in the corner for telling lies. He determined he would not be subjected to that kind of humiliation. His humiliation would be worse.

Before too long he knew what it was to be teased about his size. Always thin and underweight, he would never play sports. If he did the boys would called him 'skinny legs'. Hurt and embarrassed, he'd rush home bursting into tears as he ran through the kitchen door. His mother would listen to his story with a great deal of sympathy then quote the old proverb. 'Sticks and stones might break my bones but names will never hurt me.'

This might have been the truth but it wasn't much comfort to a sensitive nature. Then she'd add, 'It's not the size of the dog in the fight but the size of the fight in the dog that counts.' In the fourth form Frank had a teacher who seemed to dislike his pupils, Frank Houston in particular. Certainly he was insensitive to their feelings.

As he looked at his class one day he stated that one of them might become the Prime Minister of New Zealand. Frank sniggered, expecting the whole class to laugh. They didn't. The teacher, swinging round on his heel, vented his sarcasm on the culprit.

'It's all right Houston. It won't be you. You'll never amount to anything.' The stinging declaration went so deep into a young boy's spirit that he carried the wound for years. He really believed that he wouldn't amount to anything.

This experience would slip into many sermons in the future as Frank would warn parents to be careful of the statements they made to their children. The only boy in the class who did understand was the boy who shared his desk. Francis Howard had become a Christian through the Salvation Army when he was ten. His experience was so real that he witnessed to his school mates, especially the boy he sat beside. Frank and he were the best of friends but no amount of talking could win him over. After all, Frank Houston went to the Baptist church. These two boys sat together through a number of school years. Francis never gave up. If they were alone Frank would listen but if others were around he was too embarrassed to be part of the conversation on religion. Francis Howard never cared. All he wanted was for his school mates to to come to know the Lord. The friendship of the two boys continued into their teens.

Frank and Annie were pleased about it for they had warned their children that they would be known by the company they kept, and Francis Howard was good company.

In their teens the paths of the two boys began to veer away from each other although they kept in touch. Francis Howard maintained a bright relationship with the Lord by involving himself in all the activities of the Salvation Army. Frank Houston cooled in his attendance at church when he found his friends in a gang of youths. Their favourite pastimes were drinking and causing trouble. Frank always had a cigarette hanging from his mouth. On Friday late shopping nights they'd hit the town.

After a few beers they'd walk the streets passing the Salvation Army open air meeting. Francis Howard was always there but Frank Houston looked the other way not willing to acknowledge his friend. Still Francis persisted in his witnessing.

'Frank, you are wasting your life,' he'd say. 'Why don't you come to the Sunday night meeting with me.'

'Listen Francis, you keep your religion to yourself. I don't want it. I'm enjoying myself.' That wasn't totally true. He no longer told his mother where he was going or what was happening. He would come to breakfast irritable and unhappy following a night out. There seemed to be a wall round him which no one could break through. Annie knew the only thing she could do was pray.

It took a tragedy to answer those prayers. The accident happened one lunch time when Francis Howard met his father going home for lunch. Francis rode his bicycle beside the truck, holding on with one hand so that he was pulled along. It was much easier than pedalling into a headwind. Suddenly the wheels of the bike slid in loose metal, causing bike and rider to fall under the wheels of the vehicle, killing Francis immediately. Frank was devastated at the news. He still considered Francis one of his best friends.

'Why should such a thing happen to a boy as good as Francis?' he wondered. 'What was God about to allow this thing to happen or was there no God?' Frank was asking the question often asked in such circumstances. He'd find his answer sooner than he expected.

As the funeral procession passed the gates of their old school, Frank was amazed to see the teachers and pupils lined up to show their respect for a boy many of them did not even know. Frank wondered why.

Three hundred people gathered at the graveside that day. While the crowd heard the words 'We commit the body of our comrade to the grave, earth to earth, ashes to ashes, dust to dust in the sure and certain hope of the resurrection,' one young man heard something else. A voice saying, 'I want you to take that young man's place.' Frank looked around to see who could have spoken to him.

Again he heard the voice 'I want you to take this young man's place.' He shivered. No one was close enough to whisper the words so that he could hear. The third time he heard the voice. 'I want you to take this young man's place.' He realised this must be something supernatural. Everyone else was too intent on the burial service. God was calling him – he knew it in the depths of his spirit.

'You are all welcome to attend a memorial service on Sunday night at the Salvation Army hall.' Captain Spillett hoped some would accept the invitation.

'Will you come with me?' Frank asked his mother.

'Of course I will.' She did not hesitate. Here was an opportunity to get him into church again. The challenge of the voice at the graveside wouldn't go away.

Going to that service might be the answer. That Sunday night he listened to the tributes to his friend. The music, the solo 'Just For Today', and the sermon were one continuing message. 'Jesus saved Francis Howard, our comrade who has been promoted to glory. He can save you.' The message concluded, Captain Spillett invited those whose guilt was troubling them to come to the 'penitent form'.

'We will sing "All To Jesus I Surrender". Come while we sing.' The words of the old hymn carried their own appeal.

No one moved. Not even Frank Houston. He felt too embarrassed. The words of the chorus kept spinning in his mind. I surrender all, I surrender all.

Why hadn't he had the courage to go forward to the altar? Why had he been afraid of people? He couldn't answer. That night he couldn't sleep for the conviction in his heart.

He kept saying to himself, 'I should have gone forward.' After hours of struggle he climbed out of bed and, kneeling beside it, told the Lord he wanted indeed to become a Christian so he could fill Francis Howard's place. It was total commitment. A feeling in his heart told him that God had heard his prayer. Life would be very different. His mother also knew there was a change.

'What's happened to you?' she queried as he sat down for breakfast next morning.

'Last night I gave my heart to Jesus and after work I'm going to tell Captain Spillett. Annie was delighted. Captain Spillett was also delighted. He would care for this convert until he was established, but not coddle him. He involved new Christians in Army activities immediately, basing his philosophy on the Scripture 'If thou shalt confess with thy mouth the Lord Jesus Christ . . . thou shalt be saved' (Rom 10:9).

'You've made a wise decision. Now I want you to meet me here on Friday evening at seven o'clock and we'll go to the open air together,' Captain Spillett told Frank.

'I'll be there.' Frank committed himself without realising what would be involved.

Chapter 3

BLOOD AND FIRE

'Frank, it's your turn to give your testimony.' Captain Spillett looked straight at him. Frank glanced round the open air ring. Those bandsmen had been Christians for years. Why didn't the Captain ask one of them to speak? After all, it was only five days since he had made that decision kneeling beside his bed. Five wonderful days. Already he knew in his heart he would be a preacher but he wasn't ready to preach yet. Besides, his old mates were standing a few yards away chanting, 'Salvation Army saved from sin, all going to heaven in a kerosine tin,' or for a change, 'Salvation Army all gone barmy.'

He shouldn't have told Alex Bryson what he planned to do that night as they cycled into town. His old friends were already saying, 'That's the end of Houstie.' The bandsman standing next to him gave him a little push of encouragement, sending him halfway into the ring. He felt that he had better do the rest willingly. He stumbled over his words.

'I've given my heart to Jesus and I am glad I have.' He wanted to sing and shout. Speaking in the open air hadn't been as difficult as telling his boss and work mates. His Christian boss was delighted but the rest decided to knock religion out of him before it could take root. They were not going to work with a religious 'nut'.

'You mean you won't be swearing round here any more?'

'That's right and I won't be smoking any more either.'

Frank meant it. They applied pressure by trying to force a lighted cigarette between his lips while they held him on the ground. Frank spat as hard as he could. They tried again. Once more Frank spat it out. At last they grew tired of this game. Instead they rubbed rotten cauliflowers in his face and threw him in the creek to 'put the fire out'. But the fire didn't go out.

Giving his life to the Lord meant total commitment for Frank. Immediately he plunged into the life of the Corps as a Salvation Army soldier. Proudly he stood in his new uniform under the yellow, red and blue flag for the simple enrolment service in which he promised to be true to God and the Army. He had enlisted in an army which proved to be the best training ground he could have had. This was warfare. You didn't question orders.

From then on Sunday was a full day beginning with 7.30 a.m. knee drill as the early morning prayer meeting was called. Home for breakfast and back for the ten o'clock open air and the eleven o'clock holiness meeting. Afternoons were occupied with Sunday School teaching. The day finished with an open air and evening meeting. There were few week nights free. Tuesday was Corps Cadets, a youth training class where they studied the Bible.

It was also in this class that Frank first learned to conduct singing, prepare talks and memorise five Bible verses a week, skills which enabled him to be more effective in many areas of ministry. Wednesday was band practice and there was always an open air on Friday nights and a youth meeting on Saturdays. Frank wouldn't miss any of these no matter what else was on. The Army came first.

'You might as well take your blankets,' his father told him. His parents could never understand this kind of commitment. From the beginning witnessing was a normal part of Frank's christian life. His first convert was an old alcoholic. Many had tried to lead him to the Lord but the old fellow wouldn't yield. Frank didn't know this when he first talked to the derelict.

All he knew was a compassion for this wreck of humanity. He already knew that William Booth, the Army's founder, always told his people, 'Go for souls and go for the worst.' This old man must surely be amongst the worst.

On Sunday nights old Fred leaned against the shop front swearing and cursing while the open air was in progress. When the band marched back to the hall for the meeting, 'Old Fred' staggered along behind them. He knew the hall would be warm and he liked the music. How much of the sermon the old fellow grasped Frank could not tell, but when he put his arms round the dirty, lonely old man, he listened.

'Fred, Jesus loves you. Won't you come to the penitent form and give your life to Him?' This time Fred allowed himself to be led to the altar where he flooded the floor with tears of repentance. He never touched alcohol again. Instead he became the 'colour sergeant', carrying the flag in front of the band. The fires of evangelism and the wonder of what God could do in a person's life burned in Frank's spirit.

These beginning days were not all easy going. At first God seemed to surround him with a fence which kept the devil from him. When it was removed there came a flood of temptation and difficulties. In spite of his resistance, when his workmates tried to force a cigarette into his mouth he didn't find it as easy to give up smoking as he had expected. He'd throw the cigarettes away but as the craving increased he'd go back to find them. This was a problem he decided to share with his youth leader.

'Why can't I give up smoking? I've prayed about it and it doesn't work,' he complained.

'Young man, you are trying in your own strength. Trust the Lord to help you. Don't throw them away.

Keep them in your shirt pocket and when you are tempted take authority over them in the name of Jesus,' she told him.

Frank loves to declare that if a smoker didn't take another cigarette he'd never smoke again.

Gradually he found spiritual battles easier to win as his commitment to prayer and Bible study increased his spiritual strength. Frank knew that those who prophesied that his religion wouldn't last were wrong.

'It's only a flash in the pan,' the unbelievers said. Perhaps this stirred the stubbornness of the Irish in his nature so that he determined to press on. God had taken him up when other people said he'd never 'make it'. Captain Spillett had more faith. He encouraged Frank by giving him responsibility. His patience with a new convert was infinite, taking time to explain difficult doctrines and Scriptures. When he would encourage there were always some to discourage.

'Why doesn't the Salvation Army baptise people? The Bible commands it.' Or again, 'Why doesn't the Army keep the sacrament of communion?' Frank asked Captain Spillett.

'Well, William Booth believed that communion was no more important than the washing of feet as recorded in John 13:8-9. Besides, the use of fermented wine would be a temptation to converted alcoholics. His other problem: should women leaders serve at the table, a difficult question considering the place in society of women of that generation. He decided we must not lean on the external but on an act of faith in a divine person consciously revealed in us.'

'What about baptism then?'

'The act of sprinkling was kept for a while but it was believed that this was superseded by the baptism of the Holy Spirit. The Army introduced a dedication service when parents brought their babies as Mary and Joseph took Jesus to the temple.' The explanations satisfied Frank.

Nine months flew by. Frank wanted to give up his job so he could serve the Lord in a full-time capacity. Captain Spillett needed someone to help in an outpost church he'd started in a suburb. The door now opening into the ministry was closed six months later. The second world war was grinding on, requiring more men. The dreaded call-up notice arrived. Surprisingly Frank passed fit to enter camp. He determined to take his stand for his Lord from the beginning.

In camp, Frank found himself in a tent with four other members of his old gang, including Alec Bryson, the boy who had lived next door. The weather was snowy, the kind of weather which tempted a fellow to jump into bed before reading the Bible and praying. Frank resisted the urge. It was now or never to take his stand. This was where he'd get boots and pillows thrown at him for sure.

He prepared himself as he knelt to pray. Silence hung heavily in the air as four mouths snapped shut on the blasphemy which had been tumbling from their lips. Frank sat on his bed as he opened his Bible.

'What's that you're reading, Frank?' It was Alec Bryson.

'The Bible.'

'Then read it to all of us,' Alec ordered. That night led to Alec's salvation.

Time rolled round for the boys of his platoon to go overseas. They were given inoculations in readiness. One by one the men collapsed until all were hospitalised. That faulty batch of serum saved the lives of this platoon for most of the others who went to the front from that company didn't return.

Frank struggled for months to regain his health. In the meantime he received his discharge from the military which left him free to return to work in the Salvation Army. He was sent to assist Alf Herring, officer in charge of the country town Corps of

Carterton. Alf was a man who loved the Lord with his whole heart. From him Frank learned that being spiritual didn't replace a sense of humour or practical Christianity.

Alf frequently helped his neighbours repair their cars. Leaning over an engine was a good time to share the gospel.

'You see, Frank, when you're halfway through a job they know nothing about they can't tell you to quit, so they have to listen.'

Alf's wedding day was getting close. As soon as his new wedding uniform arrived he decided to try it on.

He'd no sooner slipped into it when he heard the yelping of a stray dog under the house. The beast had been annoying the two men for some time.

'Frank, you go out the front door and I'll "duck" out the back. Between us we should be able to catch it,' Alf said, grabbing the broom as he ran. The dog shot out from under the house and leaped the fence. Splash. It landed in the neighbour's slit trench, dug as a bomb shelter but now full of green, slimy water.

'Hey, Frank, help me over the fence. I'll have to get that dog out or it will drown.'

Frank pushed Alf up but Alf went right over the top into the filthy water with the dog.

'Damn it,' he exclaimed as he threw the dog out. Frank convulsed with laughter.

'That's strong language from a man who doesn't swear.'

'Shut up and come and help me out.' Alf's voice was full of laughter. 'Well after all a merry heart doeth good like a medicine and uniforms will dry-clean,' he concluded.

In this church Frank met Mrs Tyler, an eighty-year-old widow who delighted to inspire young people to serve God. Of all the stories she told as she rocked gently in her chair, Frank loved best the one about her husband.

'He'd place a chair in the middle of the kitchen where I was working. There he'd kneel to pray, thumping the chair at every request he made.

'The longer he prayed the louder he shouted, the more he thumped. But he knew how to touch God,' she said. '"Make me a terror to evildoers," he'd shout again and again.' Her old eyes gleamed at the recollection. 'You know, he'd go out into the garden on Mondays when the women in the street were hanging out their washing. He'd call out loudly, "Lord, save that wicked Mrs Smith. You know she's drinking again." Yes, she gave her heart to the Lord. He won everyone within earshot. You see young man, nothing, nothing is achieved without enthusiasm.'

These words illustrated many of Frank's future sermons. He carried that enthusiasm into Bible College for six months' training. The war had not yet ended in July, 1945. Men not at the front were regarded as cowards but this did not deter Frank. God's call was the important thing as he worked hard in preparation for the ministry ahead. Nothing people said would divert Frank from his calling.

It seemed that everyone marvelled at Frank's experience except one – me – a student of the 1944 class. Ours was a fleeting introduction. So this is the fellow they are making the fuss about, I said to myself not realising that this man would upset all my plans a year later.

Frank found college routine tough and regimented. Up at 6.30 am for devotions in the classroom. House duties until 7.30 am, breakfast at eight. Everyone had to be in uniform by nine ready for private devotions.

Classes occupied the mornings while afternoons were filled with door-to-door visitation, study or more classes. Some evenings there would be a meeting and more study. Fridays meant a half day off. Tough it might have been but students learnt discipline and self-control, lessons invaluable in the future. Halfway through the college term Frank fell victim to influenza. He had difficulty throwing it off no matter what he tried. His work fell behind. There came an ominous call to the principal's office.

'Houston, you don't seem able to cope with the work or your studies. I think you should return home to Wanganui.' Frank stared at him in shocked silence. He was being asked to quit.

'You don't mean that surely? God has called me to be an officer. Please let me stay,' Frank pleaded with tears in his eyes. The principal was reluctant to deal any student such a blow.

'Well, perhaps I'll give you one more chance but if your health doesn't improve I'll have no alternative but to send you home.'

Henry Darrel, a fellow student, encouraged Frank. 'You'll make it.' Henry knew what it was to battle against terrific odds. He'd decided when he was thirteen years old that he wouldn't go down the path his family followed for they were thieves spending most of their time in prison.

Because Henry had risen above his circumstances he inspired Frank to do the same. Graduation was looming. The students spent hours discussing where they thought they might be sent, whether it might be social work in an institution or church work in the 'field'.

'Frank, you'll go to the field for sure.' Frank thought so to. His past experience in churches assured that. A percentage would go to social work. They always did. Still, on 'commissioning' night Frank waited anxiously.

'Cadet Houston, you are promoted to the rank of Lieutenant and appointed to the Temuka Boys' Home.' He was stunned. Social work – mending shoes, cutting boys' hair – wasn't his calling. Didn't headquarters know that? Still, they wouldn't change his appointment now. He'd have to make the most of it.

Frank accepted the challenge of caring for the boys, many of whom where victims of divorce or cruelty. He felt a special compassion for the boy whose hand was scarred when his mother pressed a red-hot penny in his hand to stop him stealing. Such things were abhorrent to Frank's sensitive nature. The boys confided in him as he tried to minister love and understanding to them. He told them of the love of Jesus and some decided to follow Him. This made mending shoes, cutting hair and sometimes washing their clothes worthwhile. There were opportunities for weekend preaching in local churches.

One weekend he noticed a 'lassie' officer in the meeting – me.

'Captain Rawson, will you come to the platform and give your testimony,' Frank asked. As I did so he felt the Holy Spirit whispering in his spirit, 'This woman will be your wife.' God didn't tell me. Not then. When Frank wanted to take me home I refused his offer.

'I've made arrangements to go home with my sister. I'll stay with that arrangement.'

'You can tell her you are going home with me.' Again I refused. He wasn't going to pressure me into anything. The whole procedure was repeated when we found ourselves at the same place for supper. When I had obeyed the call of God to become a Salvation Army officer I'd decided I'd never marry. Rules and regulations stated that officers must marry officers and there were not enough men to go round.

If I had to be an old maid I didn't plan to be a frustrated one fretting over the 'what might have been.' Still, this episode disturbed me. I guessed I could have let him take me home. I was hardly back to my church when a letter marked *personal* arrived. I giggled as I read the name: Frank Houston. 'He really is determined,' I thought.

'Would you allow me to write to you?' he asked.

Well, I supposed I could do that. In 1946 the Army's rules and regulations required officers to apply for permission to 'have an understanding', which meant permission to write.

29th June, 1946

Dear Lieutenant,
Consideration has been given to your request for an understanding between yourself and Captain Rawson. This has been granted from the 28th inst. When you apply for an engagement please remember you will both need to apply with copies of medical certificates accompanying your application.

Yours faithfully,
C. Bracegirdle,
Men's Social Secretary.

Immediately I was moved 600 miles to Waipukurau, a small town in New Zealand's North Island. Getting to know each other wasn't easy when we didn't see each other more than four times in the next year. Writing letters was a poor substitute. Once our year of understanding ended we were quick to apply for an engagement. Here was another problem. Frank was still a Lieutenant.

October, 1947

Dear Lieutenant,
According to regulations, chapter six, section two, paragraph one, it is not possible to give recognition of a man officer's engagement during his Lieutenancy. You may apply again when you have been promoted to the rank of Captain.

Yours faithfully,
C. Bracegirdle,
Men's Social Secretary.

Those wretched regulations. After all, the two boys who had been in Frank's class were Captains already. It didn't seem fair that Frank should be penalised because he was in social work. We pointed this out to headquarters and then applied the pressure by phone calls. Possibly this helped our superior officers to grant Frank's promotion and the sanctioning of our engagement.

Once more sickness forced him to take time off, much to the Army's distress. That strained our relationship for a time but Frank had been told many times in college not to get out of the train while it was in the tunnel. Well this was a tunnel experience and I wasn't about to get off the train and I did my best to stop Frank doing it.

We were married on 6th November 1948. Fortunately expenses were not too great and Frank had almost enough threepenny pieces to pay the taxi when we left on our honeymoon. The rest he borrowed from the best man. Five days later we reported back to our Corps ready to plunge into our work with all the enthusiasm we could muster.

Our welcome meeting bade us 'Fight the Good Fight.' I hoped that meant against sin, not in our marriage. The Scripture informed us that 'this poor man cried and the Lord heard him and delivered him from all his troubles'. Poor we were. Delivered from our troubles – not yet.

At the end of the evening when one of the old ladies put up her umbrella, out tumbled a shower of cakes which she had stolen from the supper table. Well, I guess all our soldiers wouldn't be like that.

Within twelve weeks we had moved to a new appointment and I was pregnant. Frank seemed to be glad he was no longer mending shoes. Nothing equalled the joy of pacing the platform preaching the word of God. It was as though he had experienced the founder's wish to dangle his cadets over the mouth of hell to hear the cries of the damned. No matter how many made decisions on a Sunday night it was never enough.

The August Self-Denial Appeal was in full swing when Frank began to complain about a 'tight band round his head'. He struggled to complete the collecting but the birth of our first child diverted his attention temporarily. The baby signalled her arrival early on Sunday morning. Not today I thought. I don't have time to have a baby on Sunday. But Maureen Joyce didn't hear. Sunday evening, while father was still preaching, she arrived. Headquarters sent us a letter.

29th August 1949

Dear Captain,

We do heartily congratulate you over the birth of your daughter, and pray that she may bring you much happiness. God is good. You will know that this will lead to an increase in allowance and you will be entitled to draw five pounds ($10) per week.

Your pension fund will be increased to one shilling two pence per week and your wage tax will be 9/-. This will commence with this week's allowance.

Signed H. Goffin.

Five shillings extra would be very useful, for in 1949 sausages were one shilling a pound and eggs one and sixpence a dozen.

Frank realised it was depression causing that tight band round his head. He struggled through the collecting but the mountain of Christmas *War Crys*, an Army publication, he had to sell sent him crashing to despair. I marvelled that anyone could get so depressed. A month before our first wedding anniversary I watched Frank being driven off to hospital, eighty miles away. He was really convinced now that he wouldn't ever amount to anything.

'God, what are you doing? Don't you care?' My heart ached for Frank and for myself as I took over the responsibility of that mountain of *War Crys*. I was getting perilously close to self-pity. A total stranger pulled me out of it.

'I've been watching you visiting your husband. Mine has been in hospital three months. He's coming home tomorrow. I'm sure your husband will soon be home.' She disappeared into a train but I clung to her infectious joy. In the next two tweeks I sold the mountain of *War Crys*, packed our belongings and moved into temporary accommodation. It was two and a half months before Frank was told he could come home. The doctor ordered a year off. Who cared?

'Maureen, Daddy's coming home tomorrow.' I swung our baby round, making her gurgle with delight. At three months I wasn't sure she could possibly sense my excitement but I told her just the same. The year's leave was no rest. Frank found gardening was a poor substitute for preaching. When we returned to the ministry we were sent to a church with thirty members. Finance was scarce. Often there was not enough money to pay the accounts nor our salary but we had peace in our hearts even if I had a difference with the Corps Sergeant Major over taking my toddler to the open air meetings.

Once I feared that Frank might be killed rescuing a family from violence. We had scarcely turned the light out when the back door flung open and footsteps pounded along the passage to our bedroom.

'Come quickly. Tom's got a gun and the police won't come. He's threatening to shoot us and kill himself.' The boy shivered with fear. Frank scrambled into his uniform, fastening the last button as he ran the short distance to the house. Tom stood in the doorway, gun in hand. His mother lay unconscious on the floor, knocked out by her drunken son when he hit her on the head with a chair.

'Don't you come in here or I'll shoot you also.'
Frank had been called to this teenager before. He knew
the fellow was serious.

'Now look, Tom, don't be so foolish. You know
that God loves you and your parents do as well. Why
are you acting like this?'

As Frank spoke Tom backed into the bathroom,
locking the door behind him.

'Tom, give my your gun.'

'I'm going to kill myself.'

For half an hour the conversation swung back and
forth through the locked door. Suddenly Tom staggered
from the bathroom, flung his gun on the floor and
dropped into bed to sleep off his bout of drinking.
Frank walked home on wobbly legs.

'God, you didn't tell me that I'd have to deal with
situations like this when You called me,' Frank told
the Lord. 'I thought the ministry would be peaceful.'

Nor did we expect undeserved gossip. The misunderstanding occurred when our Australian terrier was
frequently seen sitting outside the local pub. Didn't
people realise the dog followed our neighbour and
would not come home without him?

A sprinkling of converts gave their lives to the Lord
in the twelve months we were in Hawera, but this was
not enough to satisfy a heart hungry to win souls.
Frank wanted more of God. He knelt at the altar at
officers' councils searching for the elusive experience
called Holiness. He never found it. Where was the
power of the early Salvationists?

The miraculous happenings when people fell down
in 'glory fits'?

'Lord, I long to see all you have for your people,'
Frank prayed.

In our next church God would give us a taste of His
power. The full answer was still some years away.

Chapter 4

BLOW A STRANGE WIND

December came round again with the usual question.
Would we or would we not get 'farewell orders'? We
did. Usually an officer stayed two years but probably
one was enough in a church like Hawera. Where to
this time we wondered? It was going to be a tiresome
affair packing boxes when I had only six weeks until
the birth of our second child. If only they would tell us
where we were being sent at the same time as they told
us we had to move. We were delighted with our
appointment to the small town of Levin. It was a
quiet town with a corps of sixty soldiers. Quite an
improvement on Hawera.

We quickly settled into the life of the church for it
wasn't very different from other corps. An Army
officer's life seemed to follow a set pattern and we
wondered if this would be the same. Great excitement
at the new officer's arrival with hopes of something
exciting happening, but then as the months went by a
restlessness and sometimes a spirit of criticism set in.
From then on the soldiers began to look forward to the
next change of officers. Frank was sure the frequent
change of officers contributed to an instability in the
church. Levin would be a church with a difference.

The first event in the new church would be the
Harvest Festival Appeal; the next, the birth of our
second child due ten days later.

Frank had to spend hours collecting round the
district to keep the church afloat financially. Gifts of
fruit and vegetables were arranged for a display over

the Harvest weekend and sold after a concert on the Monday night. At five o'clock that Monday afternoon I knew our baby was knocking on the door, ten days early.

'I can't go to the concert,' he argued. 'You might need to go the hospital before I get home. I'll get someone else to take my place.'

'I'll be all right. I can send for you if I need you.' He went to the concert while I checked my bag to make sure I had packed everything I needed for my visit to hospital. The baby decided to come much faster than I had expected. An hour into the concert I sent for him. Because the baby was ten days early we had an unexpected drive of thirteen miles to a hospital. Graeme arrived two and a half hours later.

We studied our people. Amongst them there were the Allisons, a mother and daughter who claimed to be Spirit-filled, and a seventy-year-old man who loved cricket and declared that silence always woke him up, and his wife. These people, with Ernie Hill, his wife and two sons, who moved into the town soon after we did, influenced the direction of our ministry. They, too, claimed to have had an experience with the Holy Spirit. This Pentecostal business cropped up all the time. Obviously it was an experience of great importance to those who claimed to possess it.

About all I knew of Pentecostal churches was the custom of greeting each other with 'a holy kiss'.

My mind slipped back to Bible College when there had been a discussion on Pentecostalism. This arose when we discovered that one of our lecturers claimed to be 'Spirit-filled.'

Certainly there seemed to be something different about Kia Ora Tyler. Her preaching and Bible teaching were alive but she didn't say much about her experience, although she told us that she believed no Christians need lose the glow of their first love for God.

'Lord show me the truth from your Word,' I prayed. I dipped into the promise box sitting on the window sill.

'I shall guide thee with my counsel and afterward receive you into glory' (Psalm 73:24). Satisfied that the Lord would lead me along the lines of Army teaching and that I'd end up in heaven, I dismissed the whole thing from my mind. Frank knew less about it until those four Pentecostal people talked to him.

Frank began to spend time praying in the quietness of the Army hall. There he could cry out to God without being disturbed. One afternoon he prayed late, unaware that dusk had fallen. Suddenly a strange sensation swept through him. Overcome by fear he rushed out of the hall, slamming the door behind him. Never had he pedalled his bicycle so fast as he did racing home that night. It did leave a deposit in Frank's life. He determined to call the church to prayer.

'I will ask as many people as can to join me at 6.30 a.m. every morning,' he told me. 'Everyone might not come but I am sure a percentage will.'

Next Sunday the week of prayer was announced to begin on Tuesday morning. Sixteen people turned up. Some stayed a short while and went on to work. Others were able to stay an hour and a half but all stormed the gates of heaven.

A week later the Holiness meeting throbbed with power. While we sang a hymn a young man dropped his hymn book on the floor as he moved out from his seat into the aisle, propelled by a hidden force to the altar, where he dropped on his knees. No one had made an altar call nor said anything which might have brought conviction. This was the Holy Spirit at work. Others followed. If this was the result of prayer the early morning meetings should continue.

They did. Next Sunday morning was even more powerful. This time the whole congregation was touched. There was no sermon, no altar call yet the people flocked to the front. Frank burst into weeping. He turned to me and asked me to carry on but I was also weeping. I turned to the organist. She was weeping. The Holy Spirit alone was in control as conviction swept the congregation. This was a totally new experience. We believed we were touching revival.

Certainly it triggered something off in the town. News of what was happening at The Army spread from mouth to ear as fast as it could be told.

One Sunday a group of Methodists walking past the hall on their way home from their own service sensed an unusual power emanating from our building. They came in to see what it was all about. They were so blessed that from then on they came in every Sunday night after their own service.

I was upset when Frank woke up utterly miserable with a soaring temperature, his body aching in every joint. Obviously this had to be a day in bed. Usually sickness turned him into a self-pitying invalid, bored to tears with time dragging. This turned out to be four days of revelation. One of our self-confessed Pentecostals brought him a book with the interesting title 'A Man Sent From God'.

Gordon Lindsay had captured what to Frank were amazing insights into the prophetic ministry of William Branham at the height of his ministry. From the moment he opened the book, Frank forgot to grumble about being sick. 'This man could tell people all about themselves, even to where they lived and their phone number. Isn't that marvellous,' he said to me.

'Sounds like fortune telling.' I was sceptical.

'But he also healed the sick and he gives scriptural references for what he did.'

'Frank, don't get carried away with such things,' I warned.

'You should read it for yourself.'

'Not me. I don't like to read about stuff like that. Those things don't happen today.' I closed the conversation and my mind but Frank pondered the possibility of New Testament-type miracles in the 1940s. Tears touched his cheeks at the thought of the possibilities. Next Sunday's sermons contained references to the book. Statements concerning the possibility of Jesus healing without the aid of medicine stirred up some objections from the congregation. Ernie Hill latched on to every word.

He had desperate need of healing. Before he had come to us from the north, doctors performed major heart surgery. His was only the second operation of its kind in New Zealand. The first patient died. The surgeon warned Ernie of the dangers but at fifty-two he was desperate.

'Doctor, you're a Christian and I'm a Christian. How about we go ahead with it. I've nothing to lose if, as you say, without it I will die anyway.'

Ernie came through the operation successfully but his activities were seriously curtailed. The family had moved to Levin to start life over again. His heart behaved normally for three months. Then he began to get pains in his chest and down his arm. The doctor's verdict was bad news. 'Ernie there is nothing I can do for you. I'm sorry.'

'Doctor, how long do you think I have. I need to put my affairs in order. I'm not afraid to die but I want to make provision for my wife and children.'

'Well, the arteries around the heart are hardening at an alarming rate. You have two months at the most. Maybe less.'

Ernie thanked him quietly. From the doctor's surgery he hurried straight to see Frank.

'Captain, ten minutes ago the doctor told me I can't live more than two months. I want you to come round tonight to anoint me with oil. I'll get some of the believing saints to join us and we'll have a healing meeting.' Frank was shocked. It was one thing to believe and preach about healing but another thing to act on his preaching.

It seemed that Frank couldn't avoid the issue. He decided he wouldn't tell me what he had to do. He didn't want any unbelievers there and I was an unbeliever with a mind as tightly closed as a can of baked beans.

By the time he arrived at the house, sixteen believing Salvationists had gathered. After some enthusiastic chorus singing, sister Allison handed Frank a saucer containing oil. He stared at it. How on earth did you anoint someone? Should he sprinkle oil on Ernie's head or pour it over him. He'd start by reading James 5:14. There was safety in that.

'If any of you are sick let him call for the elders of the church and let them pray over him, anointing him with oil.' Not much instruction there. He'd have to do something.

The Catholics would make the sign of the Cross. Perhaps that would do. Frank dipped his fingers in the saucer and drew two oily lines in the shape of a cross on Ernie's forehead as he offered a prayer of faith. Without warning the power of God sent them all reeling backwards. Ernie fell on the floor with a big smile on his face. When he'd scrambled to his feet again he picked up a kitchen chair with his left hand, raising it high above his head, something he hadn't been able to do for months.

Frank could scarcely believe his eyes. This was a spiritual dimension untapped by most Salvation Army officers he knew. When Frank went to visit Ernie three days later he found him digging his garden.

'You might be interested to know that I've been gardening, fishing and chopping the wood and it's a while since I could do that.' Ernie was ninety-three when his heart gave up for good. This forerunner of future events lent weight to the reasons some people gave for calling us Pentecostal.

Two years in this church had almost passed. Our congregation now numbered one hundred. We found ourselves on the move again. The success of our Levin ministry gave us favour with headquarters. Perhaps our next church would be a good one.

We found the Avondale corps in suburban Auckland needed an infusion of life. That would be no easy task. But with fifty people at least it wasn't as run down as Hawera had been.

On that optimistic note we accepted the challenge. Within three weeks of our arrival our second son was born. That over, life settled into the usual pattern of visitation, collecting, meetings and reports to head-quarters. Every Friday when headquarter's mail arrived Frank would 'resign'.

The church wasn't an easy one but when we exchanged our bicycles for our shiny black Austin A40 we expected life to be better. The car was a miracle. Half the finance was the unexpected result of an investment we had made. The other half came from my parents.

But that car was to bring us much anguish when accusers said we had used stolen funds to buy it.

Before too long we found ourselves at loggerheads with the 'whistling man' without knowing why. He also happened to be the Sunday School superintendent and a member of the census board, which looked after the business affairs of the corps. Apparently this man had wrecked other officers before us. Now it was our turn. He offered his resignation as Sunday School superintendent. Without hesitation Frank accepted it. His mouth fell open with shock. How dare this officer so much as think of replacing him.

From then on he made life totally unpleasant with his persecution. Not only did he whistle as he marched into the meeting but he'd sit on the front row sometimes poking his tongue out, or he would show noisy contempt at statements made in the sermon.

Amazing how such a man could preach like an angel in the open air. A continual battle began.

Frustration and depression appeared once more as the blessings of Levin were swallowed up in this opposition. The scene for Frank's second breakdown was set. He left the Army a failure in their eyes and his own. The cold reality of our situation stared us in the face. No church, no work, no home. The miracles we needed were round the corner but we couldn't see them yet. In desperation we accepted temporary accommodation with a friend.

By the time we put enough beds and the baby's cot in our one room there wasn't much space for us. We could say we had shelter and getting dressed standing on the bed developed our sense of balance. Frank found outdoor work as recommended by the doctor by becoming a 'door-to-door' salesman selling toiletries and patent medicines. He received plenty of fresh air but not much money.

The first Sunday after we left the Army we decided to go to Mount Albert Baptist church in the next suburb. We'd often listened to the Rev Cliff Reay on the radio and we'd liked what he had to say. Besides, a phone call elicited the information that they had creche facilities for babies. Our idea was to slip into the back of the church where we wouldn't be noticed.

Somehow it never occurred to us that the church might be so full that we'd find ourselves being marched up to the front seat right under the minister's observant eyes. It happened to be the monthly communion service and for the first time in our lives we partook of the bread and the wine. At that moment God was very close to us.

As the worshippers poured out of the front door we slipped out a side exit. There was no escaping the Rev Cliff Reay. He had someone waiting to detain us until he could come to greet us. That day we found a friend whose compassion steered us through further troubled waters. Soon after this service we experienced another miracle.

We'd been living in our one room for six weeks. Tempers were fraying rapidly. Frank was about to leave for work one morning when our four-year-old son did battle with the four-year-old daughter of the house. Now Graeme was the apple of his father's eye and no one quarrelled with him without repercussions. I knew our time to leave the room had come.

Frank left for work in a dreadful frame of mind while I hung out the washing. As I pegged nappies on the line I found myself crying out to God in absolute desperation.

'God give us a house today. You know we can't stay here any longer. Please God.'

Before I'd finished my prayer a telegraph boy came round the side of the house looking for me.

'Mrs Houston?' he asked. I nodded. 'A telegram for you.'

My fingers trembled as I opened it. Telegrams usually meant bad news for us. This message was simple.

There is a cottage for lease at Sunnyvale. If interested please contact me. Signed Clifford Reay.

I marvelled at the goodness of God when I remembered that He said 'before they call I will answer'. Of course we were interested. We said we would take the house without looking at it.

Now we had one large bedroom, a large lounge, a small kitchen, bathroom facilities in the laundry and a foul smell of cats. Later we were to discover that the old lady who had lived there never let her cats outside for anything. It was heaven, except for the smell. Armed with scrubbing brushes, plenty of hot water and strong disinfectant, we soon dealt with that. Our half-a-dozen forks, two blankets and old radio looked a miserable heap in the centre of the lounge room floor.

If we had put our finances beside them that would have also looked pitiful. For the first time in our lives we took out hire purchase to get mattresses to lie on. They could go on the floor meantime. Salvation Army friends supplied an odd assortment of chairs and a table. Two big wardrobes divided the bedroom.

The children slept one side, us the other. A sofa bed with sagging springs decorated the lounge room. We felt the richest people in town.

Singing filled the house. The children had trees to climb and grass to run on while father had room for growing vegetables. The Baptist church continued to be our spiritual home. When a baptismal service was announced we decided we should attend the classes of instruction. Baptism by immersion was a condition of membership in this church. By now we believed it to be the scriptural pattern for believers to follow.

'Baptismal' Sunday dawned fine and clear but the chill of a June winter day did not encourage a man with a raging fever to venture out. Frank had a dose of flu. I left for the morning service feeling the devil was at us again. Rev Reay suggested we should wait until the afternoon before making a decision about the night's service.

'I have never seen anyone suffer any ill effects as a result of being baptised,' he assured me.

By the evening Frank's fever had subsided. With a liberal sprinkling of one of his patent medicines on his handkerchief to clear his nose and a little faith in his heart we went to church. In my excitement I forgot to worry about what people were thinking concerning the strong smell of Rawleighs Ready Relief pervading the church every time Frank blew his nose.

For the first time I felt I was being obedient to the command of the Lord. Repent and be baptised He'd said. When we sang 'I'll go with Him all the way' I really meant it.

I stepped down into the water. The church was filled with a light which blotted out the congregation and the sound of the choir singing.

At the cross, at the cross where I first saw the light,
And the burden of my heart rolled away;
It was there by faith I received my sight
And now I am happy all the day.

I was and Frank seemed to be. But there was a snake in our Eden. The church made me so much at home that I was soon involved in its activities. With Frank it was not so. Struggling still with disturbed emotions and the loss of ministry, he came less and less to church until he stopped coming altogether. This was a battle of another kind. Breakdowns I knew how to handle but backsliding – no.

Prayer didn't seem to change a thing. Cliff Reay would remind Frank of the love and grace of God. Hadn't he preached about these himself? He had but he could no longer believe them. I'd go on talking about the things God had done for us. In fact I would go on talking because I didn't understand how anyone could preach the gospel and then suddenly not believe it. Nagging is the common title given to the habit. I schemed all kinds of ways to witness to him. If I asked Christians to the house Frank disappeared. His birth-day was getting close. I'll buy him a set of choir records made at Billy Graham's Auckland crusade, I decided. He loves music and he enjoyed that crusade.

But it didn't seem enough. One morning as I sat on our back steps sipping tea in the Spring sunshine, I cried to God in desperation.

'Lord I've tried everything and nothing works. What shall I do?'

Instantly I knew there was one thing I hadn't tried. God spoke clearly.

'Do nothing. Stop talking and leave him to me.' But how could God work by any means other than a wife's preaching? Still, I would keep silent. After all there was a church full of Baptists who could witness to the wanderer. God must have laughed at the narrowness of my vision but I'm sure he was pleased with my obedience.

Now what should I do with the records I'd bought. Did God mean I shouldn't give him those either. It would be an awful waste if I didn't and I had no other present. He would know why I had bought them. Yes, I would give them to him.

If he smashed them, and old 78s were easy to smash, I'd understand. Frank received his present gracefully. I felt he began to play them more out of respect for me than for the message they carried. One day I realised that one record was being played more than the rest. I found myself humming the tune while I meditated on the words.

Great is thy faithfulness oh God my Father,
There is no shadow of turning with thee;
Thou changest not, thy compassions they fail not;
As thou hast been thou forever will be.

Great is thy faithfulness, Great is thy faithfulness;
Morning by morning new mercies I see;
All I have needed thy hand hath provided;
Great is thy faithfulness Lord unto me.

Summer and winter, seed time and harvest,
Sun, moon and stars in their courses above;
Join with all nature in manifold witness,
To thy great faithfulness, mercy and love.

Pardon for sin and a peace that endureth,
Thine own dear presence to cheer and to guide;
Strength for today and bright hope for tomorrow,
Blessings all mine with ten thousand beside.*

The words were etched indelibly in my memory as I meditated on them. Strength for today and bright

---

hope for tomorrow. I clung to those words as a woman sliding into an abyss might cling to a rock. Frank was also thinking about them. God was speaking to both of us. About this time he switched jobs. A dry-cleaning company needed a driver.

'I'm sure I've got the job,' he told me.

The work was mainly picking up and returning clothes to customers.

'We want someone who knows the Remuera and Tamaki areas,' the manager said. Frank's heart missed a beat.

'Those are the areas where I've been selling the Rawleigh products,' he said. The manager showed immediate interest, giving Frank all the details of hours and salary before he terminated the interview.

'Please God let it be so,' I prayed as I thought of the holes in our shoes and the mounting debts.

Within a week Frank started the new job. God was leading us a step at a time. The children and I still went to church on our own. If only he'd come but changes were not too far ahead. He had only been on the dry-cleaning run a few weeks when one of his customers handed him a Billy Graham tract.

'Ever heard about Billy Graham?' she asked him as he handed over her clothes.

'Sure, I know all about Billy Graham.'

Marion Austin thought her 'dry-cleaner man' was a smart 'know-all'. Still she obeyed when she felt constrained to fall on her knees to pray for his salvation. She enlisted the help of two other women from her home Bible Study to share the burden. Norma Smith and Rita Fogden were only too glad to join in the praying. One morning Marion's fourteen-year-old son was soaked when unexpected rain caught him on his way to school. His teacher sent him home to change.

The 'dry-cleaner man' happened to be at the door. Marion introduced the two of them as Tony brushed past, leaving a trail of water behind him.

A few days later Tony was cycling to school when he saw Frank getting clothes out of the back of his van. It was one of those mornings when he was anything but happy. Tony wheeled his cycle round, stopping by the van.

'Good morning, Mr Houston. You look miserable.'

'Do I?' Frank was startled. Who did this cheeky young pup think he was to speak to him that way. Tony followed up the attack not caring what Frank thought.

'Do you know what you need?' he asked.

'I know what you need.' Frank snapped, his ill temper erupting. Tony ignored the reaction.

'You need to be saved and filled with the Holy Spirit,' he said.

Unaware of Frank's background, he explained the way of salvation. God had Frank's attention now.

He knew the best way to break through the morass of pain and disillusionment filling Frank's life.

'Then you are a Christian?' The question was unnecessary, for Tony's shining face as well as his words declared the fact.

'Yes I am and I'm full of the Holy Spirit.' Frank was startled by this confession.

'What church do you go to?' he asked.

'The Assembly of God.'

'You mean the one in Queen Street with the blue cross and Jesus Saves on it?'

'That's right. Why don't you come with dad and mum and me next Sunday night?'

Frank was overwhelmed by the boy's audacity. He obviously had an experience rare in many adults.

Dumbfounded by the boy's sincerity, Frank felt that he was the boy and Tony the man.

'Yes, I will come with you.' Frank was committed to an adventure which didn't please me at all.

Chapter 5

THE FIRE FALLS

'Frank, are you really going to the Assembly of God with that boy? They're a strange mob. They speak in tongues.' I was sounding an alarm.

'Yes I am. That boy's got something you and I have never had and I'm going to find out what it is. I'll sit by the door and if anything strange happens I'll be able to slip out.'

Odd that I should have been praying for two years that Frank would come back to God yet here I was objecting to the church he chose on the basis of hearsay. Well! More than that. It was the mind-closing teaching I'd had against it. Yet no one else had bothered to invite him to any church in the past year. Those critical people who influenced me were probably also filled with prejudice through hearsay. Frank went anyway. He sat by himself near the door as he had planned. A young man slipped in beside him.

'I'm David Batterham. Is this your first time here?'

'Yes.'

'I'm glad you've come. Do you mind if I sit with you?'

Frank was glad of the company. He didn't feel so conspicuous. This began a friendship which God would use as a step to rocket him into his future ministry.

As the service progressed the congregation burst into singing in the Spirit. Soft cadences sung in tongues and in English, rising and falling in unrehearsed melody. Frank had never heard anything like it.

'It was like a giant pipe organ,' he told me later. I knew he was hooked. It could have been otherwise.

Pastor Favalora from Australia was speaking out strongly against Freemasonry. Suddenly a man sprang to his feet. With eyes glaring and fists shaking he plunged straight towards the preacher, shouting all the way. Pastor Favalora pointed straight at the man.

'Come out of him you demon in the name of Jesus,' he commanded. The man crashed to the floor as though hit with a flying stone. Silence reigned. In a few seconds a subdued man scrambled to his feet and apologised to the minister and to the congregation as he returned to his seat. Frank was impressed. This was the way church ought to be. The New Testament in action. To him it was a thrilling experience, but not to me.

If that was the way God worked why didn't it happen in the Baptist church where I belonged and where I intended staying. Then the thing I feared happened about four weeks later. One Saturday morning David Batterham talked to Frank about his doubts.

'Frank, if you'd stop "iffing and butting" God would fill you with his Spirit,' David told him.

'Why don't you come with me to the Assemblies of God District Rally to hear Pastor Bruce Uren preach.'

'Fill him with the Spirit indeed,' I snorted as they walked out the door.

That night the church was packed with an enthusiastic congregation, but it was the sermon on the 'Wounded Hands of Jesus' which touched Frank. He knew he needed a touch from those wounded hands. When Bruce made the altar call Frank's hymn book dropped from his hands. Impelled by an inner force he did not understand, he made his way to the front, determined to touch God as he never had before.

He wasn't quite ready for what happened. Aware that many eyes were on him, he longed to edge behind the piano out of sight. Instead he stood in full view with his mouth wide open waiting for the tongues he'd been told accompanied the Baptism in the Holy Spirit.

Suddenly a voice in front of him said 'Shut your mouth.' He snapped it shut. Stupid man. How can I speak in tongues with my mouth shut, he thought to himself.

Another voice behind him urged him to raise his hands. He did – to chest level.

'Higher' said the voice. This time they were shoulder high. Now everybody would see him. Why couldn't they take him to another room. He closed his eyes. Perhaps if he didn't look no one else would either.

If only people would stop shouting. In that instant he determined to stop 'iffing and butting' as David had suggested. Suddenly his finger tips seemed to be gripped by an unseen force which pulled his hands high above his head. His upraised hands acted like an antenna receiving the power of God. He began shouting as loud as the rest. Now totally surrendered to Jesus, the Holy Spirit flooded his being and he burst forth in a language of the Holy Spirit.

For three hours he was lost in love and wonder for the Lord. When he opened his eyes again he stood in a church empty of people except for the pastor leaning wearily on the rostrum and David slumped in a nearby chair.

'Where are all the people gone?' he asked in amazement.

'Home to bed. It's one o'clock in the morning,' grunted the pastor.

Frank and David decided to drive round to the Austins to tell them what had happened. When they heard Frank praising God as he walked up the drive, they climbed out of bed and for another hour they all had a 'glory time' and Frank had another infilling of the Spirit. All the way home he continued speaking in tongues.

I must stop before I get to the house, he thought. But how? I don't want to stop. Hazel will think I'm crazy. Perhaps I can slip into bed without waking her up. At the sound of his step in the bedroom I switched on the light. Hadn't I been waiting hours for him to come home.

Even Pentecostal churches were finished before two o'clock in the morning—weren't they? I knew that what I feared had happened.

'I knew you'd come home like this one night,' I grunted, totally ungrateful that God had changed him. If it had happened in the Baptist church I'd have been happy.

I rolled over and left him to enjoy his 'folly', not caring that Frank had learned two things that night. No one had asked him to say pip pip pip or pop pop pop nor yet Glossalalalalalia. He would say in later years that all people got was a pip and a pop and a psuedo-baptism. He also discovered that it was not the Holy Spirit speaking in tongues. He was, although it was by the Holy Spirit's enabling.

The baptism came by faith not feelings, but with it came a consuming fire burning up the dross, enabling a power to be released which even I recognised. There was a new joy and self-assurance in his life. It was this which ultimately made me realise the genuineness of the experience. His enthusiasm grated on some of the old Pentacostals.

'It won't always be like this,' they assured him.

Well, it's been like that for thirty years. 'Yesterday's radicals have become today's conservatives,' Frank says now as he looks at some who settle for less than God makes available.

Frank spoke in tongues constantly while driving his dry-cleaning van. His spiritual growth was greater than all the previous fifteen years put together. He wondered why. 'It's because he that speaketh in an unknown tongue edifieth himself,' evangelist Ray

Bloomfield explained some months later, quoting 1 Corinthians 14:4. 'If you speak in tongues as much as that you will have more power than Mount Vesuvius.'

Another odd thing happened. One Saturday morning Frank woke up with a strange kind of feeling.

'I know something but I don't know what I know,' he told me.

'How can you know something and not know what it is?' I queried. I was completely mystified by such apparent stupidity, but David, who had stayed the night with us, had the explanation. When he brought us an early morning cup of tea, Frank told him about this strange feeling he had.

'David, I feel I know something but I don't know what I know. How can this be?'

'So you have had one of those experiences.' He didn't sound at all surprised.

'Then you know what I mean.'

'I've had that kind of experience as well. God's given you a revelation but He's missed your head and hit your heart. If you ask God He will show you what it is.'

Frank saw this as the sure way to solve the mystery. Fervently he spoke in tongues and prayed.

'I know what it is,' he shouted. 'Healing is in the atonement.'

'Didn't you know that?' David was surprised. He picked up the Bible from the bedside table and turned to Isaiah 53. 'He was wounded for our transgressions, bruised for our iniquities, the chastisement of our peace was upon Him and by his stripes we are healed,' he read to us.

'The thought is repeated in Matthew 8:17. "He himself took our infirmities and bore our sicknesses', while Peter repeats the words "by whose stripes we are healed."' David knew all the answers.

Although divine healing had been practised in Pentecostal churches since the beginning of the century, we had never really considered the idea except for that one time in Levin. Certainly the thought that Jesus died for sickness as well as sin, both of which came with the fall of man, was something totally new.

'You can accept healing like you accepted salvation,' David assured us.

'David this is wonderful, but do you think he'd heal me?'

After years of illness Frank needed assurance.

'Well, in Luke 4:40 he healed everyone. That's only one verse. Others declare the same truth,' David said.

'Lord, I've been sick all my life. Now I receive healing like I did salvation on the basis of your Word,' Frank prayed.

A warm glow swept through his body, replacing the physical weaknesses of the past with perfect health. It would be years before he experienced sickness again.

The three women who had prayed for their 'dry-cleaner man' now pressed him to come to the new church beginning in their district.

'We want you to meet Ray Bloomfield.'

'What's so great about Ray Bloomfield?' David had also spoken about this man.

'He's the pastor of our new church, an evangelist and a wonderful Bible teacher. You'd love him.' Frank wasn't interested in meeting Ray Bloomfield. He imagined some preacher trying to establish a church in his old age. The women also told Ray about the former Salvation Army officer they'd been witnessing to.

'You should meet him Ray. He's on fire for God.' Ray wasn't interested in meeting a broken down Salvation Army officer. They came face to face at a singsong at Marion Austin's home. Two shocked men looked at each other. Frank was thirty and Ray even younger. Ray's love for people and his ability to communicate immediately impressed Frank, and he found himself wanting to hear this man preach.

'David, I want to go with you to Ellerslie. I'll meet you at the hall Sunday night.' David was delighted. Frank expected by the way the people were talking there would be a crowd. There were six beside himself.

Ray preached as though there were five hundred. This man's got power, Frank decided, as he drank in every word of the message. He felt he had never heard such fantastic preaching. When the meeting was over he counted it a privilege to shake Ray's hand. Instantly they were drawn to each other in a kind of Jonathan and David relationship.

This meeting created a furore in my well-planned existence, for from then on Frank decided to travel an extra four miles to the Ellerslie–Tamaki Faith Mission each Sunday. No way was I going with him. He would drop the children and me off at the Baptist church and pick us up on his way home. It worked well for two Sundays, but on the third I walked the street for an hour waiting. Where was the man?

What on earth could they be doing in church for over two hours. The children quarrelled and every step I took as I paced up and down made me angrier until I had successfully dispersed all the blessing I had received in the service.

At 1.30 p.m. the A40 came flying along the street. I made up my mind that some things had to be sorted out and I would see they were. Frank's blessing lasted longer than mine and he was so apologetic that I decided to wait for another day. Meantime God intervened. So did the children, who wanted to go to church with Daddy.

'You are creating a divided household,' God told me. 'What do you plan to do about it?'

'What do you want me to do about it?'

'Go with Frank.' The impressions were real but not to my liking. After a brief spiritual struggle I bowed to God's will. Although the children were delighted, Frank queried my decision.

'You won't like it,' he told me.

'How do you know when I haven't been.' He was right. I didn't like it. Nothing suited my conservatism. Why would God speak through a message in tongues and interpretation when He could just as easily have spoken without the tongues. All this arm-raising was unnecessary. Unfortunately the children loved it. I decided the only thing about that church was the sincerity of the people.

This made me prepared to go another Sunday. My reaction was not much better. As Ray Bloomfield shook hands with me after the service, he sprang a question on me which I found difficult to answer.

'Have you been filled with the Holy Ghost?' he asked me.

'Yes,' I replied, remembering that I had asked God about it that time in Bible College.

'How did you know? Did you speak in tongues?'

'Goodness, no! But if I asked God to fill me with His Spirit, He would – wouldn't He?' Frank stood by the door watching. He suspected what our conversation was about and decided this would put me off for good.

We didn't discuss the matter but I determined to show that pastor he was wrong. Monday was the first opportunity to search the Scriptures. My list of verses and questions was quite lengthy but they were never asked.

Tommy Hicks, an American evangelist, was due to speak in our city and I had promised to go. There had been exciting reports of wonderful miracles in his Wellington meetings. In fact Henry and Norma Smith from the Mission had taken their four-month-old Downs syndrome baby to that crusade. They claimed that his deafness had been healed and his general condition was improved. The child could certainly hear. All this I reported to my neighbour who had an epileptic daughter.

'Why don't you bring Maria to the Tommy Hicks meeting,' I asked, even though I really didn't believe the reports myself. Try anything in a desperate situation was my attitude. In fact I was creating a whirlpool which would suck me into the very thing I wanted to avoid.

'Hazel, you'll have to stand with me if I go to that meeting.' She was most definite. Light pierced my darkness.

How could I stand with anyone when I didn't believe. 'Frank, I've decided not to go to that meeting.' His smile vanished.

'Why ever not?' I decided to soften the blow.

'Something would have to happen to me before I could go.'

A few moments later he disappeared, only to return with the information that Ray was coming over to pray for me to receive the baptism. I was trapped with no way out.

Ray turned the pages of the Bible from the Gospel of John to Acts, showing me the basis for his belief. He was getting to me with his arguments. Perhaps I had been wrong all the time.

Ray turned back to Matthew 7:9,10. '"What man is there of you, whom if his son ask bread, will he give him a stone? Or if he ask a fish, will he give him a serpent?" Surely, Hazel, we can trust our heavenly Father to give good things to them who ask, and if we ask for the Holy Spirit would God give us anything else?'

'Of course he wouldn't.' I was certain of that. Did the man think I was completely faithless.

'Well why don't you let me pray for you?' That at least could do no harm. At the crisis moment the room was plunged into darkness by a power failure, necessitating a search for candles.

In their flickering light I knelt by a chair, thinking as I did, 'what if nothing happens?' But it did. Strange syllables tumbled from my lips as the Holy Spirit was released in my soul. That same light as I had experienced when I was baptised in water glowed around me. Softly and gently the Spirit had come. My experience was so different from Frank's.

The next day I sipped tea and read the Bible instead of the usual women's magazine. It lived in a way it never had before. There were times when scoffers told us the experience was of the devil. 'Why then,' Frank wanted to know, 'did it make us love Jesus more?'

Ah, no. We were never at the mercy of the fellow who had nothing more than an argument. A new life had begun for both of us. Frank knew we had touched divine principles which could operate in our own ministry. Still God had much to teach us. There was the matter of a new pair of shoes.

'Dear Lord, I do need some new shoes. You see the holes in the ones I'm wearing. Lord they are not very comfortable with the cardboard over the holes. Please make it possible for me to get a new pair.' Frank's prayer was sincere. He'd needed new shoes for a while but there was no money to buy any.

When he went visiting he was always careful to sit with his feet flat on the floor to avoid the embarrassment of people knowing he couldn't afford new shoes. One day, when he'd been visiting the Nelsons, he forgot about the holes. As he was leaving he jumped a low fence, displaying fully the soles of his shoes with those awful holes.

'Betty, did you notice Frank's shoes? I feel the Lord would have us give him a new pair,' Dick said to his wife after Frank had left. The new shoes came as a gift from God, making it easier to have faith for a new suit.

Again Frank prayed. 'Lord, thank you for the new shoes. Now your servant needs a new suit. Those shiny patches on the one I'm wearing do you no honour.'

Once more the Nelsons were listening to God. By the perfection of their timing they could have been listening to Frank. Next time he called to see them

Dick took Frank aside.

'Frank, while I was going through my wardrobe the Lord impressed on me to give you this new suit. See if it fits you.' Frank slipped into it. He checked the length of the sleeves and trousers. Exactly right. Our faith grew by inches. Then came a small hiccup in the journey of faith. Dick phoned.

'Will you come and pray for Betty. She's sick.' Frank didn't ask what was wrong. He simply prayed in tongues all the way to the Nelsons'. He strode into the sick woman's room determined to do battle with the devil. Placing his hands on Betty's head, he prayed fervently.

'I command you devil to come out in the name of Jesus. Leave this body and let it be whole. Come out in Jesus' name,' he reiterated. I was horrified at this prayer. Frank hadn't waited to ask the problem but Dick had told me.

'Lord, unscramble that prayer. You know that Betty is threatened with a miscarriage,' I countered. What a good thing God is wiser than his servants.

The learning experience continued in prayer and spiritual gifts as Frank absorbed all that Ray said and did.

In prayer meetings Frank would kneel as close to Ray as possible so that he might experience the gushings of Ray's tongues. It seemed like a fountain had burst within, flooding his spirit until he overflowed in an unbelievable torrent of prayer. Frank yearned for a similar experience. One day when I was out he shut himself away determined to touch God.

'Lord, I want to be able to pray like Ray Bloomfield does.'

Suddenly a similar spring broke within Frank, bringing those same gushings of the Spirit. He was afraid I'd come home, breaking the wonder of it, but time proved it was not so easily lost. God dropped him from the heavenlies to earth when Ray took him to the next prayer meeting.

In 1956 these meetings were held in the home of Ray's 'in-laws'. Brother and Sister Harrison's room was packed with saints who knew how to pray in the Holy Ghost. As it reached its peak Frank experienced a welling up of tongues such as he hadn't known before. 'This must be a tongues message God wants me to give the saints,' he thought.

He gave the utterance loud and clear. Wally interpreted immediately. Without warning the gathering erupted into laughter. It rolled on and on while Frank became more and more embarrassed. Why were these people laughing at him?

The hurt thrust him into a quietness which Ray noticed as they drove home.

'Frank, what's wrong?' he queried.

'Ray, why did everybody laugh at me tonight when I brought that tongues message?' Ray burst out laughing again.

'Frank, we weren't laughing at you. That was Holy Ghost laughter.'

'Holy Ghost laughter?' Frank had never heard of such a thing. 'And I allowed myself to get upset.' It was a hard lesson. By now the meetings were beginning to grow as Ray continued to preach as though to thousands. He ministered to people in faith, seeing them saved, healed and filled with the Holy Spirit as well as set free from demons.

Frank watched and listened, for he felt this was the New Testament church continuing in the 1950s. Within six weeks of the church's beginning, Ray asked Frank to preach on Sunday morning. It was good to be preaching again. Frank had a new sense of purpose, especially as he remembered he had been told he'd never preach again. After the service Ray put his arms round Frank.

'You'll do. I would like you to be my associate pastor.' When Ray made this unorthodox approach Frank asked what he had to sign. Ray smiled.

'Brother Frank, God has a wonderful record book in Heaven. That's all we need.'

He never did sign anything but on the spot he became an Assemblies of God minister. This was eventually ratified by the executive council, and two years later they discovered he was not even a member of the Assemblies of God. Frank often said a piece of paper didn't make a minister, although he does not recommend this unorthodox approach.

The news didn't greatly excite me as I was still struggling with aspects of Pentecostalism. If someone fell on the floor under the power of the Spirit I'd do anything to walk away from the embarrassing situation. The day it happened to Frank I made my escape from the meeting using the children as my excuse so that no one guessed the real reason for my departure.

'Honestly God, what is this all about? I hate it. Why did you bring me out of the Baptist church into this? Can't you make these people and Frank quit this behaviour?' It was a long time before God answered, and then it wasn't the way I expected.

In the meantime Frank and Ray had embarked on a great adventure moving in supernatural realms uncommon in New Zealand at that time. Prayer lines grew longer as the size of the meetings increased. A thousand decision cards were signed in the first six months. On any one night there were never less than thirty decisions. No one was refused the laying on of hands so the length of the meetings also increased, but people were so involved they didn't care.

Chartered buses brought people from all over the city. They were determined to come to where there was life. Deliverance was not a debate then. It was a means by which people were set free in Jesus' name. The numbers in the prayer lines precluded any lengthy discussions or asking demons to declare their names. There was no time to pray for people more than once. The command was simple.

'Demon, I command you to come out in Jesus' name.' The prayer was offered with one eye on heaven and the other on the subject of the prayer, for reactions could be sudden and surprising. Occasionally if the men were not quick enough at side-stepping they'd be sent sprawling by the gentlest person. They learned to stand beside people, not in front of them.

Frank stood 'goggle-eyed' when he saw goitres vanish, arthritics walking and all manner of sicknesses being healed. Ray always had Frank help him on altar calls. Occasionally he would say, 'You pray for this one Brother Frank.'

One Sunday afternoon while Frank thought about his own ministry, he found himself praying, 'Lord, if you would have me enter this kind of ministry then allow a miracle to take place under my hands in the service tonight.' The Ernie Hill miracle seemed so long ago. In the excitement of the meeting Frank forgot his prayer. The crowd was so large that the prayer lines stretched down each aisle.

While Ray prayed for the people in one line, Frank moved towards a fourteen-year-old boy in the other.

'What do you want God to do for you tonight?' he asked.

'I have a collapsed lung through TB,' he said.

This seemed too big for Frank to handle.

'Brother Bloomfield will be along soon. You just pray and wait for him. As Frank turned to walk away, the Holy Spirit said, "What about your prayer this afternoon?" '

Immediately he turned back to the boy, laying hands on his head while he prayed that God would heal him. There was a hissing as the boy's lungs filled with air. Two weeks later he returned to playing football with a new lung, a miracle documented by the Greenlane hospital. News of what was happening spread throughout the city. Christians accused the men of fanaticism – wild fire.

'Better a little wild fire than no fire at all,' Ray declared. We were to repeat those words many times to our critics, but when the power of God in the meetings could be felt outside, drawing people in, why should we complain. One such instance involved a boy on his way to commit murder. As Al Fury was passing the hall, the singing drew him to the door.

All he noticed was a halo of golden light round Jack Cassidy's head. Jack, a keen young Christian, was unaware of the light although it stayed through the sermon and then disappeared. Such an unusual sight made Al want to come back.

When he did he found 'a double cure for a double curse', as he declared when he became a preacher. He needed a cure for sin, his brother Denny for sickness. Such was the power of God as He used Ray to bring revival to New Zealand in a way that had not been seen since Smith Wigglesworth's meetings.

God's method for reaching the world is people, and no one else in New Zealand could have influenced Frank as Ray did.

Chapter 6

AN UNFORGETTABLE CHARACTER

Ray was an amazing mixture of a man. In many ways an extrovert, in others a very private person who was always caring about other people and seeking a word from God. He was either loved or hated. There seemed to be no half measures. We loved him.

Ray was younger than either of us, but it was soon apparent that he could teach us many things if we were prepared to listen. Age was inconsequential. As our friendship deepened we learned to understand his idiosyncrasies. Some of his antics annoyed me until I learned to laugh with the rest.

A day in town usually meant a season of embarrassment. He'd step out of the car on a busy thoroughfare, throw his hands up in the air and shout, 'World, here I come!' It was a people-stopper, although I wondered who amongst all these strangers would care. Frank never worried. He was inclined to join in but I would slip into the nearest shop.

It was different the night they went into Auckland city together. Crowds jostled each other as they rushed to finish their late night shopping. Frank and Ray joined the crush to cross diagonally at an intersection. Right in the centre of the street, Ray paused long enough to issue an invitation to every pedestrian within hearing distance.

'Prepare to meet thy God,' he shouted. People jerked to a stop as they turned to see the audacious fellow who issued such a warning, but Ray had disappeared into the crowd.

Children's riding devices in city stores drew him like a magnet. One day he succumbed to the temptation to ride the horse outside Woolworths. Ray climbed on, dropped his 20 cents in the slot and immediately became a crowd gatherer. Onlookers laughed heartily at the sight of a grown man rocking back and forth apparently enjoying the ride. The manager was not amused.

'Get off at once,' he ordered, his face red with anger. Ray looked amazed that anyone would speak to him like that.

'Why? I've paid my money.'

'I'm sorry sir but you are too heavy for the machine. You'll break it.' The manager's voice was firm. Ray dismounted. The 20 cents had run out anyway.

'Frank, that's probably the first time some of those people have laughed in a week,' Ray said as the two of them walked away. Was Ray an extrovert by nature or because of his faith and positive confession? It was hard to decide. Frank saw a sensitive side to his nature which felt the unjust criticism often levelled at him. Perhaps Ray was the most misunderstood Pentecostal preacher of the day. There were jealousies amongst the ministers and accusations of excesses.

Ray would not be deterred from his course. 'At least the mission is alive and growing when many of theirs are at a standstill,' Ray would say. Who amongst his critics would have knelt down beside a boy scout who was measuring the footpath in an effort to raise money for a scout project. Ray offered to help. Before the boy could refuse, Ray was kneeling beside him so that he could tell him of Jesus.

When he had said all he needed to, he stood up, brushed the dust off his trousers and went off seeking others he could bless. Like the old-age pensioners waiting in a bus station he and Frank were walking through. Suddenly Ray swung round to pray for these total strangers as prophecies tumbled off his lips. Their faces lit up with pleasure.

'Thank you. Thank you very much,' was all they said as the men walked on.

Ray never passed up an opportunity to tell Indian people of God's power to change people's lives. He could converse with them in Hindustani, a language he had learned when he lived with an Indian family.

One day Ray decided to take Althea, his wife, and I shopping. Near the city we saw a car with its bonnet up and half a dozen men leaning over the engine. Ray pulled into the curb. Now what's he going to do, I wondered, knowing that to Ray points and spark plugs were all the same. He was a preacher not a mechanic. But he had seen that the men leaning over that engine were Indian.

'Can I be of any assistance?' he asked as he peered into the engine with the rest. I imagined his white suit getting covered with oil. I glanced at Althea. She seemed quite unconcerned. Who but Althea could live with this man and not be hassled.

'The engine cut out suddenly and we can't find out why,' they informed him.

'Could it be the battery or the spark plugs,' Ray asked, naming the only two parts he really knew.

'No, we've checked those.'

'If it had been the battery I could have helped but if it's anything else I can't—but there is One who can help you.' Ray began to tell them that it was Jesus. Althea and I walked on to the shops knowing that Ray could be there for another hour. It wouldn't have surprised us if he'd gone home with them to have a meal. He never could resist curries.

But Indians were not the only people Ray loved. His heart was big enough to include everybody and that included us. His was the kind of gentle love Frank needed to heal the hurt of the past. To have someone believe in him when so many hadn't was like balm to his wounded spirit.

God had brought us to a man unique in personality

and perception as well as in ministry. He only recognised one enemy – the devil who bound people with sin, sickness and deception.

The more Frank knew about Ray the more he admired him. The son of a preacher who was totally dedicated to reaching sinners for Jesus, Ray determined also to reach his generation with the gospel.

He decided the corner of Wellesley and Queen streets in downtown Auckland would be the best place to begin. But how did he get the people to stop? Ah! He'd read extracts from Shakespeare. When a crowd had gathered he put that down and produced his Bible.

The plan gathered people but not too many stayed while this raw preacher presented his sermon. Once a man did stand right through. 'I must get this man saved,' Ray thought as he shouted the unchangeable truths of the Bible. He preached for five minutes and, deciding that was too short for a sermon, did a re-run and then repeated it a third time. The man didn't move until Ray invited listeners to come to Jesus. Then he stepped forward introducing himself.

'I am the Salvation Army officer in charge of Congress Hall. If you preach like that I'd like you to preach for me.'

Ray was delighted to accept the invitation. He worked hard on a sermon for the occasion, gleaning eight pages of information from books. He set it all down in meticulous order. The night he was to preach he sat on the platform some four feet above the congregation feeling he could conquer every evil thing from hell.

Introductions over, Ray stood to his feet ready to plunge into the greatest sermon the Salvation Army had ever heard. Then disaster. Eight pages of notes drifted over the edge of the pulpit to float down to the floor four feet below. Ray was horrified.

'Lord, I'm sunk. What shall I do.' He looked up at the walls of the building. There, stretching round the wall in bold print were a number of texts. Ray had his answer. Starting with the first, he preached on every one of those Scriptures. Years later he recalls that he was never asked to preach there again.

He joined his father in the ministry. Together they developed their gifts to better serve the Lord. When they heard of revival in America they wrote to friends who were involved, asking the secret. The answer came back in the form of a book written by W. V. Grant on the nine spiritual gifts.

Well if spiritual gifts were the answer to revival they would learn to operate in them. Together they studied the first gift, then hid the book while they went out to put it into operation. They did the same with the second and subsequent gifts until they operated in them all. 1 Corinthians 12 came alive. But just as the church began to grow Ray was smitten with osteomyelitis. The pain was unbearable.

When he didn't respond to treatment the doctors knew of only one course of action to save his life. They would have to remove his leg.

'I won't sign any papers,' he told the doctors.

'You think it over. It's that or die.'

When the doctors told him, he was swamped with fear. As soon as the doctor left he gripped Althea's hand.

'Althea, don't let them do that to me,' he pleaded. 'Don't let them take my leg off. I want to trust God. He's my healer and He doesn't amputate legs.' Althea calmed him down with a promise. 'I won't. We'll believe God together.'

The doctors agreed to leave the operation for a few days. Ray felt this was a spiritual battle which he was determined to win.

'Althea, I have a vision of myself climbing One Tree Hill on two good legs, leading a crowd of people.' While Ray drifted in and out of consciousness Althea kept reminding him of his vision. 'Remember Ray. Two good legs climbing the hill.'

He clung to his picture until he walked out of the hospital on two good legs. Now there was a new compassion in his ministry. For three years he had been taking a house meeting in the suburb of Mount Wellington. Earlier he had tried tent meetings without much success. At the same time as Oral Roberts and T. L. Osborne were conducting huge healing crusades in America, Ray decided to launch out by forming a new church. He'd call it the Ellerslie-Tamaki Faith Mission.

Its one purpose was to bring the message of deliverance to the needy area of the city of Auckland. Who could know then it would reach the world. From the time we joined the mission Ray and Frank worked closely together. At first they were both engaged in secular work, but the exploding growth of the church required Ray to give up his job so he could concentrate on the ministry. It was hard work. Ray was right. Revival is fifty per cent God and fifty per cent man. It didn't simply drop out of heaven as some people expected it to.

Every Sunday night in the prayer time before the meeting, Ray would pray, 'Lord put out your silver net and bring the people in.'

'Where in the Bible do you read that God has a silver net, Ray?' Frank would ask. Ray only grinned. Silver net or not, God did bring the people in from all over the city of Auckland. By the bus load. The news of miracles and healings spread like a bush fire. Ray was an expert communicator. Bible stories lived as he retold them, applying them to people's needs. Never had we heard such a preacher.

Frank longed to have the same ability and faith. Our congregation was a happy mix of Maori and Pakeha—as they called the Europeans. On Sunday nights one of the Maori brethren would bring a greeting in his own language while Frank prepared the people for Ray's sermon with a short faith-building message. He always said it was easy to preach after Frank's word.

Ray would move in with his powerful ministry. When Ray was on an overseas trip he discovered that he was being deceived by a Maori brother with an anti-Pakeha spirit who was working to start an all-Maori meeting. When Ray told us he simply wrote: 'We need not be held back by such as he. We must progress and we do that by advancing all the time. We have no time to stay back and fight. We must push on for time is short.' Push on he did. Into realms of faith and positive confession without any of the extremes of the eighties.

'Why confess your weaknesses when you can confess that you can do all things through Christ who strengthens us,' he'd say. This had a tremendous effect on Frank spiritually and physically, acting like a stimulant on his sense of well-being.

There was something of a difference of opinion about the wisdom of turning out of bed at 2.30 in the morning to answer a call for prayer from someone with a cold. Ray would always go. Wasn't this carrying love too far? Frank wondered at the selfishness of people asking their pastor to go to them at times like these. No one minded if the person was seriously ill or if there was some other urgent reason. We had yet to learn that every need was urgent to the person with the need.

Ray taught us about giving. His supply of shirts and shoes made me wonder about his money. Not that he lived in luxury. Not at all. The home he and Althea were buying was a basic three-bedroomed house made into a charming home by Althea's clever touch. It was the obvious blessing of God which made people wonder.

'Not another new shirt,' I commented one day.' That must be the second in as many weeks.' Ray looked embarrassed.

'Well as a matter of fact I gave two to Ted. He's out of work and having a struggle you know.' Ray was always giving away money. First, he gave his tithe to the church, then gifts and a good deal more to needy people. Although Ray never let anyone know how much he gave we knew it was a tidy sum. We never heard Althea complain. She knew it would be no use.

'God always blesses a cheerful giver. "God said give and it shall be given unto you, good measure, pressed down and shaken together and running over shall men pour into your bosom",' Ray would quote. This seemed like giving to get instead of out of our love for God, a motive I could not accept. I challenged Ray.

'Does God always return to us the same as we give to Him? Does He always give money? Might he not return spiritual blessings instead?'

'Hazel, if you sow wheat you get wheat. If you sow barley you get barley. How can you get anything else but money if you sow money?'

I admitted it sounded logical. It was certainly that way for him. Not that he and Althea ever had more than they needed. It was no 'get rich quick' scheme. But neither did they want. From then on Frank decided we should tithe and the Lord blessed our giving. We gave because we loved God.

No wonder revival broke out in Ellerslie. Here was a leader who inspired the congregation by his faith and example. Frank was one who learned to stand on the promises of God. He also learned to handle critisism. When the pressure of criticism came on, and it seems inevitable in the ministry, Ray wasn't worried about it whether it came from orthodox or Pentecostal churches.

Why should he when his church was growing rapidly while many of theirs were losing ground. People knew where to find reality. The power of God was like electricity in the air, radically changing lives even as ours had been changed.

'When Peter got filled with the Holy Ghost it spoiled him for fishing and Paul was spoiled for politics. Frank, when I got filled with the Spirit it spoiled me for the churches of Christ. When you got filled with the Spirit it spoiled you for the Salvation Army and the Baptist church,' he once said to us, sharing a truth he was reasoning in his mind. Anything less than the Pentecostal experience would have been a retrograde step for us.

Frank was much more sensitive to Ray's moods than I was.

'Hazel, Ray needs encouraging not discouraging,' he rebuked me one day when I had criticised Ray's changes to the newsletter I had prepared. Frequently when we were out together we were inspired by Ray's sermonettes. These would pop out at any time and in any place. Like driving down the freeway.

'Remember the woman taken in adultery,' he'd say. 'How wonderful our dear Jesus was to her and all such today. The water blushed in His presence and became wine but never need a poor sinner blush in His presence. For them there is always reconciling love.' Ray the evangelist felt for sinners.

'The Lord has opened my eyes to the needs of the people,' he once wrote to us when he was away on crusade. 'I have stood before four hundred and fifty people here and just wept sore for them. The tears rolled down my face as the Holy Spirit touched my heart with the presence of Jesus and the needs of the people.'

Ray used the story of Frank's conversion and the way God came to us as an illustration in many sermons. He was sincere when he said, 'I know of no story to compare with your own. I have spoken at length of you and the wonderful work God has done for you and with you.' Frank said a loud amen.

He drank in every word that Ray said, storing what he could use and discarding the rest. He'd compare this with eating the flesh of fish and discarding the bones. Sometimes Frank grew impatient with Ray's lack of self-discipline. It seemed that many Pentecostal preachers of 1955 suffered from the malady.

It made us grateful for our Salvation Army experience which had taught us discipline as probably no other organisation could. This may have been a minor matter compared with his other qualities, but we always felt he could have achieved much more in the running of the church had this area of his life been more controlled.

Yet Ray could discipline himself as he proved by his custom to spend six days out of seven fasting and praying when he was on crusades. He liked to go straight from his room to the platform. That way he could not be caught by demanding people wanting their own private audience and prayer line.

Over the years Frank would also find this a problem. Such people interrupt the preparation of heart and mind for the meeting. It is also difficult to understand those who chase the preacher after the benediction wanting private prayer. By then, the preacher is drained of energy after giving everything to the ministry and the natural man craves rest. Besides, in the meeting the anointing of the Holy Spirit is strong and faith is high.

This must surely be the best time for prayer. It certainly seemed so in Ray's crusades when crowds fell under the power of God. Accusations of pushing people down made Ray eventually reconsider laying hands on everyone. He blew on people instead as Jesus did on the disciples. This also brought critisism. The only way was to do what he felt was right, ignoring what his critics said.

Even when we met together for a time of fellowship the presence of God often overwhelmed us. Our conversation was mostly about Jesus and the place He was filling in our lives. Such get-togethers usually ended with a time of prayer. One night, while we prayed, we could smell a beautiful fragrance in the room. It could not be attributed to flowers. There were none.

'Did you smell it?' we asked each other.

'Yes.' 'Yes.' 'Yes.' We all had.

'That is the fragrance of the Rose of Sharon, our Lord Jesus Christ,' Ray explained.

God seemed to be granting us new experiences all the time, deepening our walk in the Spirit. Not everyone understood.

'You Pentecostals rely on experiences rather than on faith,' our mainstream church brethren accused. Not so. With Ray's teaching we were developing a tremendous knowledge of the Word of God.

Frank found himself carried along with Ray, his faith developing while his sense of adventure in God was sharpened to the degree that any other lifestyle would have been boring. He wanted the relationship to continue forever, but God would wean Frank as a mother weans her child so that he could fulfil his own ministry. Ray saw this coming. Frank had developed the habit of taking him a cup of cold water after the meeting had ended.

'Brother Bloomfield, I want you to know that bringing you this water is the greatest honour of my life,' he said to Ray one night.

'We've lost Frank,' Ray told Althea on the way home.

'What do you mean, lost Frank?' Althea was puzzled. Ray told her about the cold water.

'He's a greater man than I am. When a man can be so genuinely humble, without pretense, he is a man of vision. He's ready to captain his own ship.'

Ray did not know it then but it would be his ship Frank would captain. Nor did we until we were all involved in revival meetings amongst the Maoris of New Zealand's Northland.

Chapter 7

BEER INTO PAINT

Bella Cassidy and Johnny Johnson, the first two
Maoris to be saved in Ellerslie, opened up a whole new
dimension in our faith and ministry. Johnny was
suffering from a mysterious illness which no one
could diagnose. His brown skin was unnaturally dark
and he'd lost a great deal of weight. Johnny knew he
was being affected by a Maori curse for which there
was no cure apart from God. He came for prayer after
a Sunday evening service.

'Ray, do you think you can help me,' he pleaded.
'The elders of my tribe have placed a curse on me and I
am dying.' His voice was weak and desperate. Ray felt
angry at the devil. Why should this fiend take the life
of a son of God. Ray and Frank took Johnny out to a
side room to pray for him. They knew that if they didn't
break this curse he would die for sure but they also
knew God's power was greater than the evil of a curse.

'Johnny, you will not die,' Ray assured him. 'God's
power is greater than any curse. We will set you free in
Jesus' name. You believe God while we pray for you.'
Johnny threw himself on his knees. Ray addressed the
demon in a loud voice.

'I command you demon to leave this servant of
God.'

Johnny was thrown into a supernatural rocking
motion as the spirit resisted. Suddenly his face lit up.

'It's gone. I felt it go.' In two days his skin had
lightened to its normal colour. In a week he had
gained fourteen pounds.

From then on Johnny determined to be 'all out' for God, which meant listening to the voice of the Holy Spirit concerning his family situation.

'It's time I got married,' he told the pastors with an embarrassed look on his face.

'Married!' Frank exclaimed in surprise. 'You're not married? What about your eight children?' Johnny grinned sheepishly.

'Well, I've just never got around to getting married, but now I want to.' He was very definite about it.

The date was set for three weeks ahead. Friends and relatives from all over the country would gather at his house, the most convenient place for the ceremony and for the hangi which would follow. The day dawned bright and fair. Preparations began early in the morning with Johnny and his friends digging a shallow pit in the backyard. In this they would cook the wedding feast.

They loaded legs of pork and a dozen chickens, kumeras, potatoes, pumkin and corn onto red hot stones and tossed in some water. Once the hangi was covered with sacks and soil so that no steam could escape, he turned his attention to preparations for the ceremony.

The children dressed excitedly in their new clothes. This was an important occasion. We arrived fifteen minutes before the service was timed to start. People were beginning to drift in slowly. Obviously, this wedding would be in 'Maori time', probably starting an hour after it was timed to. Ray went looking for the bridegroom.

'Where is your marriage licence. I need it to fill in the register.'

'Licence? Do I have to have a licence to get married?' Johnny looked bewildered.

'Yes you do Johnny. You can't get married without one.'

'Well Brother, I haven't got one. What shall we do now?'

Ray looked Heavenwards. This was the moment for some divine revelation. Everyone had come for a celebration. Well, they'd have one.

'Let's dedicate the children,' Ray suggested. The idea was taken up enthusiastically. The children stood with their parents, who promised to train them for God. Hands were laid on their heads as the pastor prayed. The wedding feast became a dedication party and nobody worried about a thing. The wedding had to wait until another day. I never did find out which day.

It was Bella Cassidy who really opened the door for us to minister to the Maoris. When she saw what was happening in the Ellerslie-Tamaki Faith Mission she thought of her own people in Northland.

Sickness was rife and sin was destroying their homes and families. They needed to hear about this Jesus who was changing the lives of so many people. She'd go on a visit to tell them. Bella's words met with a good deal of scepticism. Their prophet Ratana had performed many miracles but they stopped when he died. Bella discussed the situation with the Martins, a Methodist family who had been baptised with the Holy Spirit in Ellerslie. They agreed it would be a good idea if Ray visited the Pa.

They would ask the elders to give their permission for Ray to come. The elders questioned the Pakeha's motives and sincerity but finally they were persuaded that his visit could do nothing but good.

Ray little knew the mission field which would open up to us as he turned his blue Austin northwards. These would be amongst the most crucial meetings of his life. He was well aware the people would sit in judgement on him this first night. They would measure his love for them and the reality of the things he preached. If he failed to reach their standards the door would close perhaps forever. For the whole one hundred and fifty miles he prayed desperately.

'Lord give me favour with these people that they will hear the message which will change their lives and bring them health and peace.' After three and a half hours' driving he found the sign pointing to Waiomio. He swung the car onto the metal road leading up the valley.

Excitement ran through his body as he anticipated the extraordinary events he was sure the Holy Spirit would grant these people. The hills of the valley were lush and green but everywhere were signs of neglect. Fencing hung limply between the posts while the wires known to the locals as Taranaki gates barely contained the stock. Shabby houses dotted the landscape. The peaceful atmosphere belied the true situation of the people.

Waiomio was known to the townspeople of nearby Kawa Kawa as Drunkard's Valley. They were right. Every Saturday forty taxis loaded with beer came into that valley. Wife-beating and adultery were prevalent. That might have been all right if you were not the wife but it certainly didn't bring happiness.

'There is misery everywhere,' Bella told Ray. He believed the message of deliverance would change all this. He turned into the Martins' gate beside the meeting house.

'God, fill that meeting house with your glory in an unprecedented way,' he pleaded. He had a feeling that would happen. Sister Martin welcomed him with all the courtesy of the Maori people. She gave the man of God the best room in the house with a window looking right down the valley. To his amazement people were already arriving at the meeting house. They were coming on tractors and on horseback. Others were walking while old Zephyr cars, so loved by the Maoris, disgorged their human cargo.

Ray looked at his watch. Why, it's only 5.30. The meeting isn't timed to start for another two hours. Something good is going to happen here tonight, he decided. By the time the meeting did start the seating in the meeting house was crammed, with an overflow sitting on the flax mats covering the floor. As tradition demanded, the elders made their speeches of welcome.

'We have little to offer you,' they said, 'but we expect much from you.'

'I have come to preach the gospel and heal your sick,' Ray replied. 'We are looking for faith and where ever we find it and it is directed to God, through Christ there will come salvation and healing in his name.'

That night eighty people prayed the sinner's prayer. The prayer line stretched right round the building. He made it very clear that healing could only be expected to be permanent if they would go on with God.

'God will not heal you to serve the devil,' Ray told them.

In the move which followed, God touched every home in the valley except the Tohungas'. He kept well away, preferring his witchcraft to the gospel. Was he not the one entrusted with tribal secrets too tapu (sacred) for the remainder of the tribe to know. Besides, his close relationship with the gods gave him supernatural powers. He was not about to lose these by accepting the gospel.

'The Tohunga is angry at the people forsaking his counsel for the gospel of Jesus Christ,' Sister Martin told Ray. 'But we want the freedom of Jesus, not the powers and unhappiness of darkness.' Ray returned to Ellerslie for his Sunday meetings.

'Frank, this is revival. You must come up to Waiomio. I need your help.'

'That's impossible Ray. I can't just come like that. I have the responsibility of my job.' Deep in his heart Frank longed to go. Perhaps this was the time to voice

95

the feeling he'd been experiencing for some weeks. He was sure the Holy Spirit was prodding him into changing direction. Yes, he'd tell Ray now.

'Ray, I really feel it is time for me to return to the ministry in a full-time capacity.' Ray objected strongly.

'Frank, how will you live? You know that the church can't support you. The people have not yet learned to tithe.' We knew that Ray and Althea were living by faith themselves but the voice of God was insistent. Frank and I talked the matter over. If this was what God wanted we must obey. Anyway, hadn't the children and I lived for three months with very little income only a year ago. God had cared for us then. He would do the same now. Yet what if this congregation believed like so many who seemed to say, 'God, you keep him humble. We'll keep him poor.' Frank had believed that theory himself.

Pastors should be poor. Now God was showing him another biblical truth. He would supply all our need according to His riches in glory.

'Well Frank, like the apostles of old we will share what comes in and believe God for the rest.' Ray was again his generous self. Enough money flowed in to keep us from want, although our faith was stretched to the limit at times.

Now we were free to fully support Ray in this spreading revival. We could answer the call from other places. For weeks the men travelled between Auckland and Waiomio preaching, following up converts with teaching to establish them in the faith.

The revival in Waiomio intensified. People amazed us at the way they would sit for up to three hours on backless forms waiting for the meeting to begin. It would be another three hours before the meeting ended.

Frank or Ray began to use the waiting time for a period of teaching to ground the people in the faith. It was hard to get them established.

'I will have to hit you on the head with a bottle to send you to Heaven before you can backslide again,' Frank once said to some young men who had come to re-dedicate their lives to Christ for the fourth time. I learned some lessons of my own during this revival. One night a woman, crippled for years with arthritis, was carried into the meeting and propped against the wall.

She moaned with pain at every movement. How she sat on the floor during the sermon no one knew.

'Could God heal a woman crippled as long and as badly at that?' I asked myself, sceptical as usual. 'Well Lord, just don't ask me to be involved.' God gave me something else to do. As I sat very much the onlooker, Sister Minnie Ngakoti brought a sixteen-year-old girl over to me.

'Sister Houston, will you pray for this girl?' I was horrified, but as I was the evangelist's wife pride would not let me refuse. I offered a silent prayer.

'This has to be you Lord. You know I have nothing to give.' I placed my hand on her head, repeating aloud the words I had often heard the men say.

'Lord heal this girl from the crown of her head to the soles of her feet in Jesus' name. Amen.' Slowly I felt her head slip from beneath my hand. Horrors! She's fallen to the floor. I knew that had to be God for it certainly wasn't me. Never again would I question the phenomena even when I suspected that someone had acted from their own desire.

Had the men noticed? They appeared to be too busy praying for the crippled woman. But I forgot to be embarrassed when I heard the crippled woman scream. Her friends rushed across to where she was sitting. 'Are these men hurting you?' they cried. As she leapt to her feet they realised the Lord was healing her. The congregation clapped and stamped their feet and shouted, 'Praise God'.

The men decided the converts must be baptised before we returned to Auckland. The people took us over the rise from the meeting house to the nearest water, a stream with many deep pools. We chose a pool waist deep where the water flowed smoothly. When everyone had gathered on the banks the meaning of water baptism was explained to them. I glanced across the crowd. What is this? I couldn't believe my eyes.

The dress of the candidates was rather startling. Underpants, petticoats, dresses, jeans – in fact almost any old thing which would cover them. Why didn't we think to bring the white, lace-trimmed gowns and white trousers from the church? Yet perhaps they would have been out of place in this setting. It was a time when God looked on the heart, not the outward appearance.

The first to be baptised was a man who must have weighed sixteen stone. How on earth would Ray and Frank hold him up? They took a good grip on him, lowering him carefully into the water. As they lifted him up his knees sagged and in he went again. The two men, struggling to hold him, decided the easiest way to deal with the problem was to float him to the bank.

There he lay half in the water and half out, communing with God in a language he hadn't learned. He had received the baptism in the Holy Spirit as he had come up out of the water. Before too long the bank looked like a battlefield as others also had to be floated out of the water.

I realised that traditionalism had been by passed. I was the only one who worried about what the people wore. God certainly didn't. Some of the Waiomio people took us to a neighbouring village. On this visit we had brought some of our congregation to share the blessings of the meetings. Frank and I were given the honour of sleeping in the priest's room while those who travelled with us were given a mattress on the floor of the meeting house beside the local people.

A mother and her unmarried, adult daughter were horrified. How could they undress and sleep elbow to elbow with all these people. They pulled seats round to make themselves a corner where they could undress in private.

'Aye boy, see the Pakehas,' the locals whispered, digging each other in the ribs. Giggling spread from one to the other. No Maoris worry about 'bunking' down in their clothes whenever they sleep in the meeting house. They always sleep this way for important events like funerals or weddings. Those two women decided that campaigning amongst the Maoris was not for them.

It seemed to be the ultimate triumph of the gospel over evil when we saw a house on the hillside gleaming in the brightest red paint.

'You've painted your house,' Frank commented to the owners.

Yes, we turned beer into paint.

'Since we became Christians we've saved all the money we used to spend on beer and in six weeks we had enough to buy the paint.'

'It's better to have paint on your house than beer in your stomachs,' Frank said. Everyone agreed.

Even in revival the enemy kept up his work. The Maoris of Ellerslie were being stirred into a spiritual revolt. Ray struggled long and hard to solve the problem but Pihama, the main agitator, was adamant that they must have their own meeting. For a time the people maintained the unity between us and we hoped the danger of them leaving us was over.

'You know Frank, if they go they will soon split and disintegrate. Their self-styled leaders are too inexperienced in church leadership,' Ray said.

Before the problem was settled, God shocked us with his leading. Right in the middle of this revival Ray was called to preach in Canada for three months.

He wrestled with the invitation for a week. Leaving

the church even for a limited time would not be easy.

Then he remembered he'd said that Frank was ready to captain his own ship.

'Frank, I'm accepting this invitation to Canada. I want you to look after the church while I am away.'

Frank gasped. 'Look after the church? Ray, I don't feel ready.'

He realised the church must not lose its impetus or power. Most other Assemblies of God churches in New Zealand at that time were small and hardly recognisable as Pentecostal. The Queen Street Assembly in Auckland was the exception. By Ray's standards even that was conservative. None were seeing growth like the mission.

If it was to continue in revival power, Frank must move in the same way and with the same anointing as Ray did. On the last Sunday before his departure, Ray publicaly committed the church into Frank's care. Placing his hands on Frank's head he prayed, 'Lord give your servant a double portion of my spirit and let my mantle fall on this your servant as Elijah's did on Elisha, Frank staggered backwards as he experienced the transference of faith from Ray into his own spirit. With it came a sense of divine authority. Ray burst into prophecy. 'You shall keep your eyes on Jesus. Look not unto man but unto God.'

Frank crashed to the floor, the only time it ever happened to him. Those words of prophecy would be Frank's policy for the rest of his life. Filled with this new authority, he was ready for the challenge of pastoring on his own again.

Chapter 8

ANOTHER'S MANTLE

Even as we waved goodbye to the Bloomfields, rumblings of discontent amongst the Ellerslie Maoris grew louder. Within two weeks they had taken their departure, only to become scattered as Ray had forecast. The gap a hundred people left in our congregation was discouraging. But it didn't end there. In a month our numbers dropped from four hundred to eighty. It appeared the revival fires were dying. This testing time drove Frank to his knees.

'Brother Houston is putting on a brave front,' someone in the assembly said. Brother Houston wasn't putting on a brave front. He was following Ray's prophecy and the word in Hebrews, 'looking unto Jesus, the author and finisher of our faith'. Things would change he was sure.

But he wondered what Ray would think when he heard his congregation had dropped so disastrously, and hear he would – from someone in the congregation. Frank decided to get in first. He wrote immediately to tell Ray of this apparent disaster. The saints who had been most closely associated with Ray were already pressuring Frank. The nucleus, they called themselves.

'Frank, you should visit those people to encourage them to come back.' Although he hated losing people Frank didn't feel led to do this.

Anxiously Frank awaited Ray's reply. When it came it was in no way condemnatory.

'You explain a little about losing some while not wishing to lose any. The success of your work will not depend on how many you have lost or retained but rather on how many new ones you have added. In our kind of work we must expect many to come for the loaves and the fishes and then leave. Some will stay to help us in the fight against sin, sickness and disease. Fight the good fight. Keep the faith. Go on for the crown.'

Frank remembered his Bible College principal's words: 'We are engaged in a war and in a war there will be casualties.' Two months went by without any new people appearing in the church.

'When you preach you get what you go for,' Ray had once told Frank. Frank was going for souls and to free the captives of Satan, and he determined to preach his best no matter how many were in the meeting.

When a new family appeared one Sunday night Frank felt in his spirit that this was the beginning of a new move. The recession was over. The next Sunday there were more new families. Every Sunday after that new people came, while some of the Maoris drifted back. Soon there was standing room only. Frank realised he had the same faith as Ray to see God working in miraculous power in the lives of people.

He knew he was indeed wearing another's mantle. The atmosphere in the meetings became electric as people witnessed miracles and healings every week while the lost were still finding Jesus as Saviour. Yet all did not believe in spite of seeing the power of God at work. The congregation was tense the night a blind brother came for healing. He couldn't distinguish between light and dark since he'd lost his sight five years before.

Frank could feel faith in the man. Still he asked, 'Do you have faith that Jesus Christ will open your eyes tonight.'

'I know he will.' His voice was full of confidence.

'I rebuke this spirit of blindness in Jesus' name.' Frank spoke with divine authority. Suddenly the man pointed in Frank's direction.

'I see the Pakeha,' he shouted.

'What does he look like?' Frank asked.

'Beautiful.'

The congregation rocked with laughter but as the man counted the lights in the building and described the colour of the ties worn by the men standing at the back the laughter turned to praise. At least all praised God except one. A visitor from another denomination. The lady asked sarcastically, 'Was he really blind?' Did all believe in Jesus' day? The meeting was over and the man stepped out into the blackness of the night.

For one awful moment he thought he'd lost his sight again but he was still seeing weeks later.

The story of this miracle spread around, bringing to the meeting a lady, blind for forty-three years. Again Frank came against the spirit of blindness in the name of Jesus. Breathlessly the congregation waited for the miracle. Nothing. Frank prayed again.

'I command this spirit of blindness to leave.'

The woman claimed to see a faint light but nothing more. This time God healed gradually. It was a month before she could see clearly enough to cross the city's main street unaided. Frank remembered that the Bible spoke of the blind man seeing men as walking trees. Now he understood that God was sovereign in His dealings with people. Not all would receive miracles nor would they receive healing in the same way. Some would not be healed at all but there is no doubt that Jesus does heal today.

As the work in Ellerslie multiplied, bringing new demands, efforts were made to maintain the Maori meetings in the north. The church elders shared the responsibility by going alternate weekends to Waiomio. News of God's power was spreading fast. The Waiomio saints were arranging meetings in other villages. Frank filled these other engagements whenever he could. Many of the old people spoke little English and Frank did not speak Maori except for one phrase.

It was enough to make one old lady think he could understand the language. She'd come for healing.

'Whakapono ki Ihu Karaiti?' Frank asked.

'Yes, she had faith in Jesus Christ.' Convinced that Frank could understand, she poured forth her story in a torrent of words. The only interruption was Frank's 'aye' which made her think all the more he knew what she was saying. The interpreter grinned. He knew that Frank didn't understand any of it. It didn't matter. Frank placed his hands on the woman's head as he prayed, 'Lord touch this servant of yours and make her whole.' Her face lit up, all the evidence we needed to know God had answered prayer.

'Who said God was an Englishman anyway,' Frank would often say.

Forty miles from Waiomio was the settlement of Ti Ti. No Pakeha had been allowed into this place since a false prophet had tried to establish a new religion there years before. The ruined foundations of a temple bore mute testimony of a disaster.

The door into Ti Ti was opened when relatives persuaded the reluctant elders to allow Frank to visit the village. He was aware of their opposition and felt some trepidation as they drove onto that *marae*, the meeting place of the people, watched by the curious eyes of a group of naked children. A good congregation gathered in spite of some opposition. Satan was not about to relinquish his grip easily.

'We've come to see what the Pakeha has to offer,' the elder said in his welcome speech, though Frank was uncertain how welcome he really was.

'Lord, you'd better do something good tonight or your servant will be thrown out.'

He preached that night as though his life depended on it. Well, perhaps not his life but certainly his bodily comfort did. Faces were so serious that he wasn't sure if they understood. Was the interpreter faithful in his translation? Perhaps they are simply weighing up my words. He concluded his message with the usual appeal for those who wanted Jesus to be their Saviour to stand up.

They all stood. They must have misunderstood what I said, Frank thought. He was puzzled at the response, so he asked them all to sit down again. Following a further explanation of what he was asking them to do, he invited them to stand again. Once more they all rose to their feet.

'Do they understand what I am saying?' he asked the interpreter.

'Yes, they understand,' he replied. 'They all want to get saved.'

Now came the real test.

'Would all those who need healing come now and I'll pray for you.' Not a soul moved.

'Jesus wants to heal you tonight. Come now so that I can lay hands on you and pray for you.'

Still no one moved. Frank was perplexed. Nowhere had there been this reluctance to come for prayer. Then an elderly lady rose stiffly to her feet. Leaning heavily on a stick, she stumbled forward.

'Severe arthritis,' Frank thought. If she was not healed he'd be regarded as much a phoney as the false prophet and he would also be thrown out. He thought of his skinny frame landing unceremoniously outside the gate. 'Lord I'm a bit of a coward and I don't want to be thrown out. It's now or never. Heal this woman for your servant's sake.'

Aloud he shouted, 'I command this arthritis to leave this body now in the name of Jesus.' Instantly there were clicking sounds as the woman straightened herself. With the pain gone she tossed away her stick and marched round the meeting house. Suddenly the prayer line stretched the length of the hall. People rushed to their homes to get the sick. Two and a half hours later Frank prayed for the last person. He glanced at his watch. Midnight. He felt exhausted. Bed would be good tonight. That was when he was asked to pray for a man who had been bedridden for five years.

'Of course I will,' he replied. He wished he wasn't so willing as he stumbled up a steep hill with a dozen people. The light of the torch barely lit the rough path they had to follow, but when Frank looked at the sick man, compassion replaced his tiredness. This man needed God.

'Have you given your heart to God,' he asked. That was always the first question when he ministered to a stranger. If the answer was no he'd tell the sinner Jesus could change his life. 'You can go to heaven with a sick body but you cannot go with a sick soul,' he explained. He led the man to Jesus then prayed for his healing.

Nothing seemed to happen that night, but the next night at a meeting in the small township of Moera, that man walked into the meeting unaided. The place turned into an uproar with shouts of praise to God. Northland was aflame with the moving of the Holy Spirit. If we went shopping the assistants asked us about the healings.

Taxi drivers continued to wonder about the loss of their Saturday business and Frank knew that God had given him a measure of faith similar to Ray's. The move of God's spirit was only hindered by ambitious men who desired places of leadership beyond the call of God. One with a tremendous ministry in personal witnessing coveted the pulpit ministry God had given Frank. Against all advice given by experienced men of God, he set out for the north determined to preach in pulpit meetings.

The Maoris of Ti Ti resented his coming without invitation, closing the village once more against the ministry of Pakehas. Others in the mission caused concern. News of the problems filtered through to Ray, who had now been away six months instead of the three he planned.

Immediately he wrote with some advice.

'I have just heard of the little trouble you have had with some in the meetings. I was sure this would arise but just as sure it will do you all good. It is when we are driven to our knees that God speaks with words of wisdom.

'May I make a suggestion with regard to the situation. I am not interfering with your leadership in any way, but because we love each other I offer you a few little tips from one minister to another that may help you, Brother Frank. Nobody knows like you that behind our brother's trouble there is a definite lack of love. A man lacking in love is a dangerous man to himself first and then to others.

'You see, the harm he is doing to us or even the church is nothing to the harm he is doing to himself. We must show love to save him from himself. Some will say, "If only Ray knew." My beloved Frank, love is the answer. It never fails. All else will. Temper every wind that blows with mercy. I have absolute faith in your judgement. Sometimes we must shut out the advice of our friends and judge with love and understanding where they would judge on what has been wrongly done. God does not deal with us after our sins.'

He moved on to speak about a prominent woman in the church. 'She will make a better friend than an enemy and every effort should be made to show her real love and understanding. We do not want enemies within if we can avoid them.

'Since the loss of her husband she has found her escape in the realm of service to God, but being unlearned, she is in danger of making a shipwreck of her life also.'

Fortunately, wearing another's mantle didn't mean copying his ways or aping his thoughts. Frank's understanding of love differed from Ray's. He was sure these people would do exactly as they wanted, regardless of anything he might say. He did nothing. But there were principles Frank and Ray knew were necessary to the success of God's work. While unity and love were essential they needed to be bound together with loyalty. Ray also wrote about this.

'I do love the great Ellerslie-Tamaki Faith Mission. I see in it the great ideal as far as evangelism is concerned. Also I see in it the blessedness of working together in unity and oneness. When I think of the way ministries function together without the old "green-eyed" monster coming up, I praise the Lord. Frank, we have proved there is a body ministry and my motto is "every joint supplieth".

'Many will pretend to want to help you and make offers for the so-called glory of God. They seek the secret of your oil. Believe me, dear Frank, that when so many other ambitious folk come along they will bring the work to a standstill.'

It would be lack of loyalty which God used to confirm the end of our ministry in Ellerslie.

Frank felt it was time to move out into the community by having a crusade in the next suburb. He booked the High School hall and our people distributed leaflets advertising the meetings. Only one elder, who was also the treasurer, had doubts, but he seemed to go along with the rest. The saints prayed that God would reach down to people as we reached out to them.

In the middle of these preparations, Frank flew four hundred miles south at the invitation of the Lower Hutt church to preach over a weekend. As I waved goodbye I had a strange feeling that this was no ordinary weekend of meetings. I prayed for Frank with an intensity I rarely felt. Then I thought I saw the reason for the invitation. They were going to call him to be their pastor.

I must be wrong. We hadn't heard that Pastor Midgely was leaving Lower Hutt. The idea wouldn't go away. Was this the Holy Spirit or my own imagination? I wasn't sure. Well, I'd know soon enough. When Frank arrived back he chatted on about the thirteen who were saved and the sixteen filled with the Spirit.

'Stop it man,' I thought. 'Come to the point.' Finally I interrupted him.

'When are we moving?' Frank looked aghast.

'How did you know they'd called us? Did someone phone you?'

'Then it is right.'

'Yes. After the meeting the elders asked me to meet them. I was sure I had offended them in some way and they were going to tell me off. Instead they told me Bob Midgely would go to Japan if we accepted a call to replace him. I came away convinced I'd be writing back declining the invitation. Now I am confused. But how did you know?'

'I guess the Holy Spirit told me.' At least that was a more spiritual answer than to say I just knew.

Thoughts for and against the move whirled round in our minds for days without any clear leading. Why should we leave a church in revival for one with only forty members, peaking at sixty on special occasions? Who could possibly care for Ellerslie? Why leave our new house, the first we'd been able to call our own. Ray had moved to Canada in 1955 and in 1957 he still showed no signs of returning. He wouldn't be pleased if we left. Besides, there was the coming crusade in Panmure. We decided we wouldn't tell anyone, not even the children, until we had some clear guidance. The whole church would be rocked if the people thought we were moving on. Frank began to fight against what he somehow knew was inevitable.

'I think I'll talk to old Brother Thompson,' Frank announced one morning. 'As the secretary-treasurer of

the Assemblies of God he will know what is best.'
He'd once told Frank to stay with the work during
Ray's absence.

Pastor Wallace Thompson had a special interest in
the mission and Frank felt he was bound to tell him to
stay.

'You know, Brother, while I was flying home I
decided to stay here. When Hazel said she knew about
the call before I told her I felt more confused than ever.'

The old pastor looked over the top of his glasses and
in his deep, penetrating voice said, 'Brother Frank, I
think you should go.' Frank reeled at his words. That
wasn't what he wanted to hear. Could this old man,
who prostrated himself before God every morning,
have got his guidance wrong for once? Frank was still
restless and unsettled in his spirit when the telephone
rang. It was Henry Smith.

'Frank, I am ringing on behalf of the elders. We
have decided that the Panmure crusade is off. We can't
afford it so I've cancelled the hall.'

'You've what!' Frank was shouting.

'Cancelled the hall.'

'Henry, what are you saying. You mean you have
cancelled the crusade without discussing it with me?'

'That's right.'

'Henry, love and unity are necessary for the progress
of God's work, but so is loyalty. Is this being loyal?'
Biting anger was in Frank's voice. Who's running this
church he thought, as he slammed the phone on its
hook.

'Hazel I'm going into my room to fast and pray
until I find the mind of God.

'I don't want to be disturbed for anything, even if it
takes a week or a month to find the answer. He disappeared through the door with his Bible in his hand.
Well that will make the cooking lighter for a day or
two I thought. Five minutes later he was back. 'Get
out the boxes. We are moving. See this.' He pointed to

his Bible. 'Get thee out of the north country into the south,' I read. Who could argue with this confirmation.

The people in the mission were upset.

'Frank, you can't leave us. It's obvious that Ray isn't coming back and who else has a ministry like you two?' Our thoughts exactly, but God had said go.

Frank wrote to Ray immediately. He trembled as he opened the next Canadian letter.

Dear Frank,
Loving greetings in the name of Jesus.

The news of your intention to leave Ellerslie was indeed a shattering blow. I know of no other way to describe my feelings.

However, I wish you God's blessing in your new post. I do trust you will prove to be a great fighter in the cause of Christ. Never look back. Always keep firing and never trust the enemy. I am sure you will give full proof of your ministry. Lots of things are on my mind as I type this letter. I am wondering about the saints at Ellerslie.

You must know as I do that except there be strong evangelistic ministry there it will not grow. Churches grow on evangelism as far as numbers are concerned. Who can meet that immediate need? I trust you will see that some kind of satisfactory arrangement is made for the ministerial needs of Ellerslie.

Frank, go with my blessing. Remember 'greater is he that is within you than he that is in the world.' Give them the works down there and have great Holy Ghost revival.

God be with you dear ones.
Love, Ray.

The umbilical cord was broken. As Frank put the letter down he glanced out the lounge room window. The sun was shining on a field of ripe cocksfoot grass. Suddenly it appeared to be blown by a gentle breeze. Every seed head seemed to turn into a human being.

'I saw a multitude of people praising God,' he told me.

Like a deep inner prophecy, God said: 'I will cause you to raise up an evangelistic centre in Lower Hutt that will finally have an outreach to the world.

'It will touch a multitude of people.'

While Frank had his vision I drowned the floor with my tears at the thought of leaving these people who had helped us to dramatically change our lives. Well, I could be thankful that for this move I wasn't pregnant. Our fifth child was three months old.

Chapter 9

THE SOUTH COUNTRY

With the removal truck loaded and the children assured that the drivers would feed the cat, the dog and the ducks tucked comfortably in a side compartment (not all together of course), we turned the A40 southwards towards a new challenge.

Our call was for two years but the sceptics said an evangelist couldn't pastor a church for that long. In Frank's mind there was no conflict. He'd had sufficient pastoral experience to blend the two. He was totally convinced that every evangelist needed a church base. Besides, he knew that two years would not be long enough to establish the evangelistic centre of the vision.

We faced the thirteenth of December 1959, with a real sense of anticipation. The Red Cross hall used for the services was tucked away between more imposing buildings down an unimportant side street. It was without windows and short on paint but sixty people gathered in our first service to worship God. Old people were plentiful – young folk very few – but the spirit of worship and praise gladdened Frank's heart.

Suddenly a high-pitched scream shattered the harmony of worship. Frank stood with mouth agape and I jumped three inches off the seat. Granny Diamond was praising God again. The rest of the congregation worshipped on undisturbed.

We discovered that this diminutive seventy-year-old worked up to this pitch every Sunday morning, staying there till she ran out of breath. The children dubbed her the local fire engine. Here was one problem we would need to solve. Any visitor coming to the meeting would be put off for ever. But Granny Diamond proved to be one of the greatest prayers in the church. In fact the old folk were the ones who undergirded the work by their dedication to prayer. To them must go the credit for much of what happened in the future.

Christmas broke into an already busy schedule. For the first time, Frank had decided we should go to the annual Christmas camp and national business conference. The business sessions, held in the afternoons, were enough to deter any newcomer. Pastors sat with a copy of the constitution on their knees and their tongues ready to argue irrelevant points. For five days the delegates wrangled over, what Frank decided, was inconsequential to the lives of people.

For a whole week they argued and there were only thirteen churches represented. Delegates were asked to nominate men for the executive council, the controlling body of the Assemblies of God. Frank was amazed that someone should nominate him. Unknown, though he thought himself to be, he decided to let his name stand. He was surprised to be elected.

Then the feeling was replaced by a sense that God would use him to bring the movement into greater evangelism than it was pursuing. He would accomplish more than that. God would use him to release the fellowship into freedom in praise and worship. He determined that he would also work towards getting the business sessions streamlined so that less time would be taken up with unnecessary argument. His opportunity came when he was appointed superintendent some years later.

This half Irishman was a fighter, making life uncomfortable for some members of the executive in the cause of progress and freedom. Once or twice he was known to walk out of an executive meeting to prove a point. Following Frank's election, Ray Bloomfield wrote once more.

'So now you are on the executive of the Assemblies of God. That is wonderful. Push for real old-time Pentecost and refuse to settle for less. Remember God's desire is signs, wonders and miracles, in all our churches . . . Frank, keep preaching deliverance and love. If you want to see Christ glorified and people set free you will have to preach the power-packed message of deliverance from sin, sickness and disease. Lead the people out of the muck and the mire. Jesus is the way out and the way in. Praise Him.'

Sometimes Frank wondered if the movement could revive.

Yet when pastors of independent churches tried to persuade him to also go independent, the awarenesss that God had some special purpose for the Assemblies of God kept him where he was. The antagonism towards these independent groups by some of his fellow ministers left Frank puzzled.

'How can you have fellowship with pipe-smoking ministers in their fraternity when you will not associate with born-again men from other Pentecostal streams?' he'd ask them. 'Many of those ministers are not even Christians.'

There seemed to be no satisfactory reply. He is still puzzled by the narrowness of such a point of view. Although the work of the executive would require much time, Frank's main vision was still the church. At the February board meeting, Frank presented his vision for Lower Hutt, a city of eighty-five thousand.

'If we are to make an impact on Lower Hutt by reaching the people for whom Christ died, we must get out of the Red Cross Hall,' he told them. 'We must go to where the people are. I've been asking God for direction and I feel we must take the town hall for a

115

crusade.' The men's eyes popped wide open and their usually vociferous tongues remained silent for a full two minutes.

One man spoke at last. 'Take the townhall. That seats twelve hundred.'

'Where will the money come from?' asked another.

Frank knew he had to bring them to the point where they shared his vision. Without that there could be no success. Seed thoughts dropped into the discussion took root until the whole board agreed to fully support the plan. They began to pray and organise the church to work as one body in this major crusade.

Our limited financial resources were stretched to the limit as we did everything humanly possible to let people know we'd be in the townhall. A nine by six foot hoarding appeared on our front lawn where everyone on passing trains could see it. Motorists stopped to read it, including the city council inspector. He banged loudly on the front door one afternoon.

'You are not permitted to erect hoardings in residential areas,' he told Frank. 'You'll have to take it down.'

'I will,' he assured the inspector. 'I didn't realise it was illegal.' Sometimes Frank Houston is slow to act and the crusade was over before he removed it. The night of the first meeting, the caretaker at the hall said, 'I don't suppose you will be expecting many tonight. People don't come to religious meetings these days.'

'We'll see.' Frank was non-committal but he did confess to some inner doubts as he watched to see if any new people came in. They did – eight hundred of them. Enough to fill the ground floor.

When the invitation was given, a young man rushed down the aisle and up the steps to the platform in his eagerness to find God. He was followed by twenty-two others. A Brethren boy was healed of a severe back complaint. The people's faith was extended as they saw the possibilities of evangelism. 'You are welcome to come to a study on the Holy Spirit in the Red Cross hall on Wednesday nights,' Frank announced.

Many did come and stayed to become members of the church. Four weeks later our congregation was up to ninety. The treasurer scowled as he saw our bank balance going into the red. 'Taking it big for God,' Frank called it.

'You see, people and churches dry up and become narrow; bound by miserable concepts which stop them going out where the people are with initiative and boldness,' he said. 'The command to evangelise is already there and you don't need to have any special guidance from God to do it.' Once the crusade was over, the treasurer breathed freely again. The bank balance had turned black.

The meetings had aroused considerable interest in the baptism of the Holy Spirit amongst other churches. A searching group of young people from the Baptist church asked to come to the house for a discussion on the subject.

'You will be welcome,' Frank assured them. 'When do you want to come?'

'Tonight.'

'Fine. I'm looking forward to meeting you.'

Eight young people hungry for God asked questions for two hours before Frank prayed for them. The next Sunday morning they occupied the front row in the morning service. 'Ah! I must tone down the service this morning so as not to offend the Baptists,' Frank thought.

'I'll sit with Granny Diamond to keep her quiet,' I offered. That morning the spontaneity of praise carried Frank into the heavenlies so that he forgot about those young people on the front row and I couldn't silence Granny. Suddenly he remembered. 'What about the Baptists? They'll really be upset.'

Frank opened his eyes. They stood with hands raised, praising God as loudly as the Pentecostals. There would be misunderstanding because of such incidents. Those young people didn't leave their church but others did. Some Christians accused us of sheep stealing.

'We don't steal sheep. We grow grass,' Frank answered the critics. Frank found an assistant when he had a rare bout of sickness. Margaret Skilleter, the church secretary, suggested asking Trevor Chandler, a former Baptist, if he'd preach in the emergency.

'I'd be glad to,' he told Margaret. Trevor found a new church home and Frank had a man loyal and skilled to lead the church without missing a beat when he travelled. Soon the hall we used was uncomfortably full.

It was unwise to go out and then return during a meeting for the heat and smells were overpowering. We needed a building of our own. It had to be central and near transportation. Stan Carter, a board member, walked door to door calling on property owners in an area suitable for the church. He found a property with the correct zoning and a price we could afford – £5,000 ($10,000). We bought it. There was some cash in the bank but the rest was a step of faith.

An architect worked on plans which the council passed without any problems. We were ready to demolish the old house on the site when the council called a halt.

'You can't build on that land. We want to put a street through there. We'll buy it for £7,000 ($14,000).' Sold. Two thousand pounds wasn't a bad profit in six months, but now we had to find another site.

'God, what are you doing?' Hadn't He made the whole scheme possible? Kate Wilmshurst, one of our prayer warriors, told Frank of a vision she'd had.

'We were worshipping in the old Commonwealth Covenant Church.' That seemed an extreme idea, for that church would never sell to us. Our membership included a number of folk they had excommunicated and that didn't make them very friendly. It was a big building right at the gateway of the city.

Then Charlie Wilmshurst discovered that the city council had bought it for road widening but had changed their plans. They had offered it to the Salvation Army. Charlie Wilmshurst, a former Salvationist, was sure the Army would turn it down as it wasn't suited to their purposes. Within two days he phoned with the news that the Army had declined the offer. Immediately Frank contacted the town clerk.

'I hear the Commonwealth Covenant Church is for sale. Is that right?' he asked.

'Are you interested?'

'Yes, I am.'

'I was about to lodge an advertisement in the newspaper as you phoned. I'll hold it until you have seen the property,' the town clerk said. Frank didn't waste any time in looking over the church and the hostel which went with it.

'This would suit us perfectly. How much do you want for it?'

'We will not accept less than $60,000,' the town clerk replied.

'Can I have the keys over the weekend to show my congregation?' Frank could hardly contain his excitement. There had been no time to consult the church board. Nor did he want to for the moment. He'd come to feel that God never works through committees: he chooses a man (though the man may need committees to help him). Besides, two of the board members had suffered at the hands of this church. Would it hold too many painful memories for Clarrie Potbury and Stan Carter?

That Friday night the church was engaged in a half night of prayer. When it was well under way, Frank tapped these board members on the shoulder.

'Bring your wives into the back room. I want to show you something.' Frank held the keys in front of the men. 'Guess what these are.'

'Well, what are they?'

'The keys to the Commonwealth Covenant Church. It's for sale and I believe God wants us to buy it.' The two men looked at each other.

'Only last night we discussed how wonderful it would be to occupy our old church. It was built for the glory of God,' Stan said.

'Let us leave the prayer meeting to the Holy Spirit and go round to look at it,' Frank said. As they stood in the building, tears coursed down the cheeks of both men as they realised that God was giving them the opportunity to regain the building they had sacrificed so much to build.

Frank felt the first fence had been cleared, but there were other people with painful memories of the place. How would they react?

Frank told the congregation at the end of the morning service the next Sunday, inviting them all to come and see the property. He felt a little like Joshua leading his army round the city walls as we marched one hundred and twenty strong over the bridge leading to the building. It nestled on the river bank across from the main shopping district, an excellent position. A sense of excitement pervaded our little group as we stood in the empty church praising God.

It seemed so large, but we wanted it. We prayed that all obstacles would fall before us – mainly the $60,000 one. Old Brother Moeke knelt at the altar, letting his tears fall on a spot sacred to him before excommunication had forced him from fellowship in this place. Sister Wilmshurst shook as she praised God for her vision and its complete fulfillment. Frank saw his evangelistic centre and I saw engagement and wedding rings and other forms of sacrificial giving which had made the building possible in the first place. We claimed it for our own, knowing it would be a challenge for our faith. Frank phoned the mayor on Monday.

'We'll take the church,' he said.

'You had better make an appointment to come and see me,' the mayor said. He was an astute businessman. 'It will cost you $60,000. Do you have that much money?' the mayor asked.

'Yes of course we do.' Frank didn't tell him it was still in the bank of Heaven. He believed God had shown him the city council would carry the finance themselves.

'We will probably have to call tenders as it's public money.'

'You can do what you like but we will win the tender.'

'How can you know that?' The mayor looked astonished.

'We know that God has given us the building, so anything you do is by the way.' The mayor laughed.

Frank was leaving for America a few days later. Before his departure he met the mayor getting into his car in the town. 'Mr Mayor, what are you doing about our church property?' Frank asked him.

'There is a council meeting tomorrow night and I will see what I can do.' They offered us the building for $60,000. Some of the board members wanted to accept their offer, but Frank knew God had said pay $55,000 and that was what he offered them. They accepted.

With interest-free loans from church members, as well as some gifts, our finances stood at $28,000. With that amount of money in hand we felt the finance shouldn't be hard to raise. Frank left for the States not knowing where we'd get the rest of the money. We didn't count on the Government's credit squeeze imposed at that moment. No one would lend us the money. Frank rested in the Word of God.

While we were trying to raise the finance, the council had allowed us to furnish and prepare the building for our opening. We'd been able to buy an organ the Seventh Day Adventists had ordered but couldn't pay for. Frank didn't tell them we had a church we couldn't pay for.

When we had to tell the council the money was not forthcoming, they were in a predicament. If what they had done became known there would be a public outcry. If they evicted us the same thing would happen. They carried the finance for five years.

We had the centre. Now we needed five hundred people to fill it. The whole project was a faith venture and to meet it wisdom from God was needed. Had this been simply mental assent to an idea, it would have been a very risky business.

'Faith is taking hold of the revealed will of God before it ever happens and believing it into manifestation. A revelation from God – a *rhema* out of *logos*,' Frank told his people. Thus there was confidence and action in the steps they took. God did not have to be talked into anything.

Frank launched into evangelism. He'd hold some tent crusades. They were the most fruitful but not without their problems. There were Wellington's notorious gales, and vandals who drove their car into the tent doorway during a meeting. None of these things stopped people flocking to the meetings from the beginning. Whole families were saved. For a week a woman living on the hillside listened to the singing drifting up to her. One night she dropped her knitting on the table and reached for her coat.

'I can't stand it any longer. I'm going down to that meeting,' she told her husband.

That night Mrs Janes found peace in Jesus while I found an angel who would minister to the pastor's family by doing the ironing every week for some years. But the devil actively stirred up trouble by inciting men whose wives had been converted. They threatened to burn down the tent. Others determined to stop the meetings by complaining to the authorities about excessive noise.

Neither stopped the crusade nor prevented God drawing sinners to Himself. Our gains were considerable. Now the roles of evangelist, pastor and teacher became intertwined in a perfect balance so that new people became disciples established in the faith. Evangelism and teaching would always be Frank's aim.

'One without the other is a lop-sided gospel making people prone to deception and a church with stunted growth,' he'd say. 'People can become self-centred, always wanting to get and never giving anything to God.' Pastoring new people meant answering some difficult questions.

'Should my wife and I separate now that we are Christians?' Keith Hamilton asked. This was a thorny one requiring a search of the Bible, consultations with other ministers and reading up on some of the old authorities on the subject. Research led to another question. Was divorce the only sin God did not forgive? Frank wrestled with the problem by much prayer until he felt God had given him clear direction.

'Are you happily married?' Frank asked Keith.

'Yes we are.'

'Then why break up a second marriage with all its attendant pain for both you and your family when nothing can be achieved by it?'

'But isn't it living in adultery to be married to a divorced person?' Keith wanted desperately to do the right thing at whatever cost.

'Did not God blot out all your sin when you committed your life to Him? Is divorce the unpardonable sin? I don't think you should leave your wife, but you must make the final decision,' Frank told him.

Keith decided that God did not want him to divide his family. This question would finally become a major debate as more divorced persons came into the church. Odd how a woman strongly opposed to remarriage sat beside this couple for some years taking communion with them without objection, yet left the church when Frank officiated at the wedding of another divorced person.

The difference? She didn't know divorce had been involved in the first situation. Frank came to the conclusion that each case must be decided on its own merits in the light of our understanding of what God was saying. That decision had a price tag we would only discover some years further along the way when divorce hit our own family. This wasn't the only problem which needed solving.

Increasingly Frank became aware that the system for electing the church board had many shortcomings. Some members actively campaigned for election. The families of others suddenly began appearing in church every Sunday. Frank realised that the bylaws required a person to have attended the meetings regularly for eight weeks to be eligible to vote at the annual meetings.

When a new member asked how she should vote as she really didn't know any of the men nominated, Frank knew why he had to work with some who were unsuited for the task. Careful study of the Bible suggested a more scriptural way. Sunday morning sermons touched on church government as Frank taught the principles of appointment instead of elections.

Before the annual general meeting, Frank tactfully approached each board member and his wife to explain the proposed changes. At the annual meeting he presented the proposal to the members as they had to vote on the changes.

'If you pass the proposal you must realise this will be the last vote you will have,' he told them.

They passed the motion with an overwhelming yes. He felt that he should select the board himself. Who better knew the type of men needed to advance the work and handle the business affairs of the church. Not 'yes' men, but fellows who knew God. Men who shared his vision and would not sit across the table at every board meeting glaring at the pastor and opposing every move he suggested.

Harmony was an essential ingredient for success. The congregation didn't look for the required qualities. They voted for their friends or by guesswork. No wonder the support needed wasn't always forthcoming. One tried to get the members to vote on our leadership at an annual meeting when it wasn't even on the agenda. This system of hiring and firing pastors which hurt so many men of God was, to Frank, as unscriptural as any system could be.

'We are not here to fight each other. Our enemy is the devil,' Frank declared. Only one felt that he could not accept the change. Frank regretted his resignation for he was a good man, but he was determined the new way was for the best.

'The pastor will become a dictator in this situation.' The accusation was levelled at Frank.

'The executive council is a church's security,' Frank assured them. 'Anyone with just cause for complaint can go to them and, if need be, they can take whatever action they deem necessary.'

The executive council was not a body of men who agreed on everything, but they were in agreement when they needed a new superintendent. Ralph Read, the current superintendent, had accepted a call to a church in Australia. He was a gifted organiser who had given strong leadership to the movement in New Zealand. The Lower Hutt church wondered anxiously who could replace him.

Our board offered to pay his salary if he'd stay as superintendent in a full-time capacity. Ralph felt that would be out of the will of God. Frank, now assistant superintendent, found himself elevated to the position. Neither of us wanted that. There was already so much to do in the ministry but we yielded to what was assuredly the purpose of God. We knelt in dedication while Ralph Read prayed for us with laying on of hands. Both of us were aware of a special sense of God's calling into a phase of ministry which would release the fellowship into a period of growth.

It grew from fifteen to forty churches as the bonds of traditionalism were broken by spontaneous praise and worship, often accompanied by dancing.

'Frank, if you start dancing in this church I'm leaving,' Trevor Chandler declared. Sylvia, his wife, wasn't sure. Trevor had been totally loyal to Frank during his years with us and the thought that he might leave because of such an issue was unbearable. Who could lead the church in Frank's absences like Trevor?

'You know Frank, with Trevor at the helm everything continues as though you were here,' I'd often say. The dancing broke out one Sunday when Trevor was away preaching. Sylvia told him about it on his return.

'That's it, I'm leaving.'

'Just a minute,' Sylvia said calmly. 'I started it!'

There was no settling down in the church, for now the Holy Spirit told Frank to establish a Bible school to fill the gap left by the closing of the Assemblies of God college.

The ministry in New Zealand was suffering from a lack of trained people. It would also be part of the vision to reach the world.

'Lord, give me one hundred men. One hundred men dedicated to you at whatever the cost. Then we will make a real impact for the kingdom.'

The aim of the college would be to train young people to evangelise the world. Academic excellence would be important but secondary to the development of their spiritual lives. No way must the fire of the Spirit be doused, although education must not be despised. Students came from Samoa, Fiji, Indonesia, Australia and Sri Lanka. They returned to those countries and more.

'These are your spiritual sons,' the Spirit whispered.

'They have laid aside fears and frustrations for the hopes and challenges of faith, but they know God is their partner,' Frank declared. 'God is faithful.' Some of the students shared the thrilling experience of a two-week crusade (which stretched into six) in the city of Hamilton, eighty miles south of Auckland. Praying for people until the sun came up was a common feature of this crusade as multitudes came for prayer.

A desire for a similar ministry was birthed within them but they had to find their own. Students from other cultures not only received training but kept alive the church's vision for missions. Local ethnic churches helped as well.

The Samoan brethren organised an evening to portray life on their island. Samoan songs and dances had the congregation clapping and swaying. One song in particular stirred the people until they praised and worshipped God. The Samoans laughed. Max Rusmussen, the group's leader, didn't have the heart to tell the people the meaning of the words.

Minoi, minoi, minoi; Pei o se toi.
Wriggle, wriggle, wriggle like a worm.

It was an old Samoan dancing song.

All this was but a preparation for ministry reaching from the south country to God's 'sheep which were not of this fold'. Frank would be amazed as God sent him to other cultures.

Chapter 10

OTHER SHEEP

'Frank, there's a telegram under the door.' We were checking the unoccupied manse, something we hadn't done for weeks. 'It's from Australia.'

'Who would be sending a telegram from Australia?' He tore it open, read it and passed it to me.

'Would you be available to preach at the Toowoomba Christmas camp commencing Boxing Day?' wrote Tom Whiting. 'Will you go?' I asked.

'I'd love to if it can be arranged.'

'Can I come with you?' I'd been planning to go to Australia in September but I was still a long way short of the fare. 'By Christmas I will have enough money.'

Australia fascinated both of us. Acres of deserts, thousands of kangaroos, cuddly Koala bears – though some friends had said that they were not as nice as people thought. And snakes.

I didn't think of people. Frank did. He'd heard of the needs of the church in this vast country. He wanted this to be the time when God would again meet the people's needs with 'signs and wonders' following the ministry and I would be privileged to share the experience. I'd book seats on the plane. They were not to know that I needed $200 more for the fare.

Frank's would be paid of course. Somehow I knew I'd be in Toowoomba at the Yukana Vale camp in Queensland. Australia, here I come. When Frank boarded the old Lockheed Electra I was with him, as well as our two boys. When we touched down at

Sydney airport, Brian, with his nose pressed hard on the window, said, 'Can't see any snakes, Dad.'

But there were other creatures. Not at the airport but certainly in Queensland. Myriads of flying beetles, mosquitos large enough to carry a man off, or so the Australians said, and flies. Persistent little beasts which stuck to our faces in spite of our efforts to drive them off. When Frank stood up to speak the first night he put his hand on his hip and quickly removed it as he felt something wriggle.

'Everyone, bow your head and close your eyes while we pray.' As heads dropped in prayer Frank brushed his hand across his hip, sweeping the creature into the air over the audience. How was he to know that Christmas beetles were not included in the list of Australia's dangerous creatures. Frank prayed earnestly for the blessing of God to fall on the meeting, regaining his composure as he did so.

With this introduction over Frank forgot the insects as he plunged into preaching. That night Jesus healed a pastor's wife of a long-standing back complaint. He prayed for an eleven-year-old boy suffering from asthma.

When he vomited all over the floor Frank realised for the first time that sickness can sometimes be the result of demon possession. He looked at the Scriptures. Yes, the ministry of Jesus and the Apostles confirmed this.

Day after day Yukana Vale, Aboriginal for Valley of Praise, rang with the praises of God's people as revival swept the camp. Older saints compared the meetings with the revival in the early years of Pentecost when The Good News Hall in Melbourne echoed with the voice of an English evangelist, Smith Wigglesworth. The news of God's power at work in this camp spread throughout Australia, opening many doors for ministry in the future.

Our final meetings were in Inverell, New South Wales. The temperatures soared to one hundred degrees farenheit, almost more than two 'Kiwis' could bear.

'Whew! I'm glad I'm not going to hell,' Frank muttered.

Again God touched the lives of people with His miracle power, but one miracle never came. Henry Gallus, a well-known Pentecostal, had two problems. He needed new teeth and he didn't believe in people falling under the power of God. He came once more for prayer asking God for a creative miracle. He fully expected new teeth to grow. When Frank prayed for Henry he fell face downward, nose pressing on the floor boards. I could scarcely suppress my giggles as I watched his toothless mouth speaking freely in tongues. Henry was big enough to admit he had been wrong.

May that year brought a second visit to Australia. Frank had heard of the revival which had broken out in Launceston, Tasmania. Pastor Worley, the evangelist responsible, needed to return to America, leaving two Australian pastors, Norman Armstrong and Gerald Rowlands, with the responsibility of the work. They felt that another evangelist was needed to keep the momentum rolling. But who? Norm remembered Frank's ministry in Toowoomba. He could do it, he thought.

As a result of Norm's phone call Frank packed his bags once more and flew to Tasmania believing that the evangelistic vision God had given him for Lower Hutt was exploding into something bigger than he had dreamed. The revival in Launceston had not subsided but increased.

'This is an entirely new Holy Ghost work,' Frank wrote. 'It is an experience indeed to see the great importance these people put on things which to you and me are everyday occurrences. There had been no manifestations of the Spirit in the public meetings until last Sunday when I brought a tongue message and interpretation. The congregation were speechless and overawed at such a glorious thing happening in their midst. On Sunday there were three tongue messages and interpretations by new Spirit-filled Christians. It appeared God was taking over the police force when seven policemen and their families turned to the Lord.

'More healings have occurred than in any other campaign I've conducted,' he told me in a letter. I knew Frank was happy. The friend who told me I might as well leave the suitcases out was right. The next time I packed them Frank was off to Apia, Western Samoa, to dedicate a new church.

Calvary Temple's congregation overflowed to the outside. Each window was filled with curious faces trying to see what was happening on the inside. The choir of a hundred island voices singing in harmony brought tears to Frank's eyes, but when he saw these lovable, friendly people coming to receive Jesus as Saviour the tears flooded forth.

'Most Samoans go to church on Sundays,' Frank wrote. 'But their ministers smoke and some drink. The churches have bingo parties to raise funds but the people don't hear the glorious gospel message. Praise God the Pentecostal fire is burning and hundreds are turning to Christ; two hundred and forty-six in this crusade. They are leaving dead churches for life in Calvary Temple.'

And life there was as the cook found out. With the help of Billy, a twelve-year-old boy, he was busily preparing the meal to be served at the end of the service.

'Billy, I'm out of salt. Will you get me some from the house.' Billy ran off but decided to look in on the meeting on the way past. As he peeped through the door Frank looked straight at him.

'You need the Holy Ghost,' he said. Straight away he prayed for him. When the cook realised that Billy was a long time coming back he went searching for him. He found him lying flat on his back on the floor speaking in a strange language oblivious of everything.

'I don't know what the *Palangi* (white man) prayed but I know I can hear perfectly,' a man, deaf for twenty-four years, told Pastor Fatialofa, Calvary Temple's pastor. The evangelist's greatest farewell gift came from a young man who put his arms round Frank's neck; his tear-stained face against his cheek. In broken English he said, 'I have no money to give you as a parting gift, but as you leave Apia I give you the gratitude of my heart for introducing me to the Lord Jesus.'

In Nadi, Fiji, Frank learned the sacrifice expected of the missionary when he had to sleep on boards covered by a blanket. Then after a sleepless night to be called at 4 a.m. for a prayer meeting was more than he could stand. Pastor Nathaniel had to pray alone. Frank had plenty of time to pray before the first meeting began in the evening.

The market place buzzed with excitement as the meeting progressed. Nearby a denomination opposing Pentecost organised a rally of their own. Frank chose to ignore them. He was not in competition with anybody but there to preach the gospel, which he did with the aid of two interpreters translating the message into Hindustani and Fijian. When Frank shouted they shouted. When he jumped they jumped.

People, unable to resist such enthusiasm, came running from the opposing rally to see what was going on. Many of those who gathered were Hindus and to take a stand for Christ meant excommunication from family and friends. But still they came. The sick flocked forward for prayer and so did the curious onlookers. It was hard to tell the difference as the sick were healed, although a fourteen-year-old boy kept shaking his head at the noise as he was delivered from a deaf and dumb spirit.

Frank's overseas journeys began to read like a travel brochure when, in 1966, the church sent him on a fact-finding mission which would circle the globe and lay a foundation for future ministry. He was to look at the way missions and Bible colleges operated. Although the church paid his fare he would need money to provide shaving cream when his supply ran out, and perhaps a film. The bank teller looked aghast that anyone should consider a six-month journey with only $200 in his wallet.

Even that amount scraped our bank account clean. 'Be sure to pray for me,' he told the family as we said goodbye. 'Write often.' Six months apart from the family sounded a very long time and as we followed his travels on a world map it looked a very long way. His first stop was Manila in the Philippines. What would he do if our old friends, Dal and Dorothy Walker, were not there to greet him? But they were.

Frank knew nothing of culture shock but now he experienced scenes which stirred him to the depths of his spirit. Dal took him through the stifling heat to a large Roman Catholic church.

There, towering above the worshippers, was a statue of the black Christ and a lesser statue of the apostle Peter. A seemingly endless line of people crawled in from the street and down the aisle until they could kiss the feet of the Christ. Some were covered in sores and others were sick. Indignation welled up in Frank's heart while tears rolled down his cheeks.

'Dal, I'm going to tell these people that Jesus can heal them with out all this humbug.'

'Frank, you can't do that. You'll get thrown out.' The scene still challenged Frank twenty-two years later. He travelled on to Mindanao where he slept on the floor with the rats and then to Calamba to visit a Bible school with fifty-one men and women 'who seemed possessed by an unquenchable fire for God', he said.

133

'The singing is wonderful with mighty praise and worship. Although they have little of this world's goods, they enjoy the abundance of God's grace,' he told us in a letter. There was opposition from another church. They organised a film show right beside us. Finally they lost much of their crowd to the preaching and the sight of God instantly healing a blind man and restoring the hearing of a young boy.

'These were only two of many miracles and I cannot say how many gave their lives to Jesus.' Frank's letters were inspiring.

Dal and Frank boarded a Jeep for the long haul back to Manila. This was the first time Frank had travelled with two trussed pigs, filthy dirty and continually emitting ear-splitting squeals. Beside him sat a young boy holding a rooster. Frank reached over to stroke its feathers. Poor thing. Someone will probably be eating it soon, he thought. Well it wouldn't be as bad as bird's nest soup or some of the food he'd scraped out the window to the dogs when his hostess wasn't looking.

'Every day is quickening my pulse for missions,' Frank wrote home. 'This country's needs are so great. Poverty, and worst of all, its idol worship are terrible, as is the hypocrisy of the established church. I would like to see some of our dedicated young men on this field. Dal and Dorothy are two of the best missionaries I know. To hear Dorothy praying in the early hours of the morning makes me weep. She is a real intercessor,' he wrote.

Hong Kong was a further shock. As the plane dropped down between the high buildings the density of Hong Kong's housing became a reality. In 1955 the slum area of the squatter's village still existed and the Walled City was at its worst. Frank's meetings arranged for Hong Kong had fallen through.

Instead he found himself speaking in a mission to drug addicts. Kay Locke, a petite slip of a woman with a fearless faith in God, was the chief missioner. Her husband worked to keep them and to support the mission.

Frank fought with his emotions as he walked down the stairs into a small hall jammed with fifteen to eighteen-year-old drug addicts. The words of 'Take the name of Jesus with you' and 'There's power in the blood' sung in Chinese had new meaning for Frank.

Kaye wrote his text on a blackboard. 'Jesus said I am the way, and the truth and the life' (John 14:6). Seven emaciated and trembling scraps of humanity reached out to that life in a grim struggle to escape the horrors of addiction. The narrow, dark alleys of the Walled City were filled with danger yet Kaye walked fearlessly guiding Frank through the dangers.

'I've never seen anything so terrible. The stench and filth are nauseating,' he wrote.

'Rats run round our feet and children, seemingly hundreds of them, play amongst the filth. We slipped on the slime as we walked along miles of alleyways. What a hell on earth.' Frank's spirit was grieved as he thought of the complacency of the people at home.

'Drug addicts lying everywhere: on the ground, on wooden shelves – anywhere they had had their fix. Most were motionless, like corpses – oblivious to everything.'

'I leaned over one precious teenager for whom Christ died and wondered if he was dead. Then I saw the artery pumping in his neck. Could you have looked and not wept?' he asked in a letter to the church.

They climbed steep stairs to an upper floor. There, in a well-kept and spotlessly clean 'house' about five by five feet, a radiant eighty-four-year-old Chinese lady lived. She had committed her life to Christ four years ago.

On this day she complained of toothache, but when they looked she hadn't a tooth in her mouth but a tiny splinter of tooth working its way through her gum.

'Come Granny, I'll take you to the dentist.' Kaye took her arm, helping her along the dark alleys to a brightly lit doorway. The dentist's surgery was spotlessly clean and well set up. Here a young American Christian missionary dentist devoted his life and talent to helping the poor.

In the final meeting in Hong Kong a convert sang happily, but the twitching and restlessness of drug withdrawal had begun.

Could anything be worse than this, Frank wondered as he boarded the plane for India. But India was as bad or worse. For the first time Frank saw people sleeping on the streets. 'Poona, in 1966, was a city of millions and not one church of any denomination preaching a clear message of "ye must be born again", let alone the wonderful truths of the full gospel so precious to us,' Pam and Graeme Truscott, our friends from New Zealand, told Frank.

Food parcels from home made it possible for the missionaries to live. Frank renewed his commitment to make Lower Hutt a springboard for missions. A centre reaching out to the world. He loved these Indian people but hated the conditions they lived under.

'India is a country like the gods they worship,' Frank says. 'But note the measure of prosperity the believer experiences compared with the poverty of so many unbelievers.'

The spirit tree next to Graeme Truscott's home kept on shaking and whispering, holding people in bondage, but the Holy Spirit was bringing light and life. Bangalore, a city five hundred miles south of Bombay, was Frank's final stop in India. And it nearly was final. Here he ministered in the Assemblies of God Bible College by day and in public meetings at night. American missionaries the Rev and Mrs Dillingham, pastors of the local church, and the principal of the college, the Rev McDermott, had been crying to God for a real move of the Spirit.

'It is so difficult for the people of Southern India to receive the baptism,' they told Frank.

On that first night God moved in power and five were baptised in the Holy Spirit. Immediately the atmosphere in the college changed. Conviction spread to another student who came on the altar call and cried for two hours.

'What's the matter?' Frank asked him.

'I'm a third year student and not even saved.'

'Then why do you live a lie?'

'Because this is somewhere to live and I can get food. It will be different now.' Frank was shocked by a third student who never smiled. At last Frank asked him why. 'My father is a Presbyterian minister and he told me I'd get good training in this college but I don't believe in Pentecost,' he confessed.

'You will receive the baptism in the Holy Spirit at 9 p.m. next Friday,' Frank told him and that was the way it was. This young Presbyterian fell to the floor and rolled like a barrel for two hours, speaking in tongues the whole time. The public meetings at night were crowded. At the end of one meeting a young man shouted out, 'What right have you to preach this Jesus to Indian people?' With eyes flashing, face angry and fists clamped by his side, he pounded down to the altar.

'He's going to kill you,' the Holy Spirit whispered. Frank took two strides towards this hostile man. With forefinger pointing straight at his enemy Frank began to speak words of knowledge revealing the hidden sins of the young man's heart. He took several steps backwards, Frank following up his advantage. Suddenly the man dropped into a chair, yelling as loudly as he could, 'Jesus, I didn't believe in you. Now I do. Save me from my sin.' Frank reluctantly turned his back on India. He wished he was going to Madras with Graeme Truscott instead of Israel and London.

Still, two days' rest in the land 'where our dear Lord ministered, died and rose again', as Frank described

Israel, was like a refreshing shower. Frank prayed 'not my will but thine be done' in the Garden of Gethsemane as Jesus had done. Disgusted with the hypocrisy and false information of the place, he longed for London and some good, honest British life. From the moment he touched down at Heathrow he appreciated the friendliness of the people. This is like coming home he said to himself. But the November weather was foggy and cold.

'They haven't had any summer and now winter is setting in,' he said in his next letter home. 'But I love the country although the feeling of defeat invading the political scene appears to be invading the church. This is a tragedy and I find it very depressing.' By the time he visited England again it was 1985 and the spiritual climate was changing. England was awakening to life in the Spirit, although some pastors could not accept what was happening. Others, straining to press into God, wanted to leave the Assemblies of God.

'Stay in the fellowship,' Frank urged them. 'Stay the same as I did years ago and let God use you to bring life in Christ.' Some stayed. Some didn't. 'Standing shoulder to shoulder is the best way for the church to do battle with the devil if it wants to set the captives free.'

Frank found America seething with evangelists but he wondered what they were accomplishing. When he talked with Billy White of Tonawanda, NY, about meetings in his church, the first question Billy asked was how much did Frank charge?

'Nothing. I don't put a price on the gospel.' Frank was amazed at the question. 'But you must charge something. All evangelists do.' 'I don't,' Frank replied.

Six months had flown by as Frank turned towards home. How was he ever going to settle into a small church programme. 'My sights have been so lifted and my vision so enlarged I doubt if the church will be able to take one half of what I envisage for the future,' he said. The vision stretched to other nations and the challenge of increased missionary giving.

'Whatever culture you are in the people are the same, with the same problems and the same hurts. And they love the liberty of the Lord except for a few old diehards who refuse to get out of their rut.

'It's the ministers who stop revival, not the people,' Frank accuses. He has been startled at the lack of Pentecostal power. In so many countries even as late as 1988 the missionaries have left strong, evangelistic churches, but they are often legalistic with no knowledge of how to operate in spiritual gifts. This didn't stop Frank. He feared no man and moved as the Holy Spirit directed.

'I've been asked to speak at a youth camp in Sydney,' he said, showing me a letter which he'd received that day. I appreciated his anticipation of the meetings as I knew that Frank loved ministering to young people. He organised his church meetings well ahead of time and bought his tickets. Then the blow fell.

'Sorry, we are not permitted to have you come. The State executive has ordered us to cancel your visit.' Members of that council would eventually become good friends, but at the time they could not see what God was seeking to do. Why argue. Once more Frank believed that he would see God's justification.

'It's only the Western world with its sophistication which does not receive freely from God,' Frank alleges. 'These other countries have no such inhibitions.'

The fulfilment of the vision still continues as the challenge of other cultures continually confronts our society. Frank has a heart for God's 'other sheep'. My right arm sometimes grows weary of waving goodbye, but we did make a commitment never to withhold each other from 'the war as good soldiers of Jesus Christ'.

Chapter 11

MAGNIFICENT MARRIAGE

Somewhere between Frank's comings and goings we've managed to build a marriage. Ours would be the perfect marriage. During our engagement we had discussed the ministry, in-laws and children: there would be four. We had them all fitting a neat pattern.

We entered into marriage intending to fulfil all the covenant the Salvation Army asked us to sign. The wedding service began with the officiating officer reading these articles of marriage from the Salvation Army book of ceremonies, 1934.

(a) We do solemnly declare that we have not sought this marriage for the sake of our own happiness and interests only, although we hope these will be furthered thereby; but because we believe that the union will enable us the better to please God and more earnestly and successfully fight and work in the Army.

(b) We hereby promise that we will not allow our marriage in any way to lessen our devotion to God, our affection for our comrades or our faithfulness to the Army.

(c) We promise whether together or apart, always to do our utmost as true soldiers of Jesus Christ to carry on and sustain the war.

(d) We promise that we will use all our influence with each other to promote our constant and entire self-sacrifice in fighting in the ranks of the Salvation Army for the salvation of the world.

To all of this we said a loud amen and we have never withdrawn that commitment, except we were finally called to see it outworked in the Assemblies of God, not the Salvation Army.

To have and to hold, from this time forward, for richer for poorer. We could only be richer for we had nothing of this world's goods to lose. I can still hear the sound of those threepences Frank used to pay the taxi driver as we set out on our honeymoon.

Ten hours later I made a discovery. The man I'd married was good at getting his own way. Before I had time to get up the stairs he'd scrambled into bed, thereby claiming forever the side he wanted to sleep on.

But marriage wasn't going to be the simple thing we'd planned. In our commitment we were one but, in personality we were two very different natures. We would have to work at blending his Irish fire and determination with my independence and stubbornness. God alone knew how we'd need those qualities in the future when our weaknesses became our strengths. Besides, we were a good balance once we'd learned to understand each other. Fortunately we didn't enter marriage with the idea of changing each other.

The Salvation Army's belief that men and women were equal in ministry encouraged what I believe should be in marriage – a sharing of responsibility, and share we did. He preached one service and me in the other. The main difference for me between being a single officer and married was that now I did all the housework and the cooking. Frank pressed his uniforms.

'You might get double creases in the trousers,' he'd tell me.

We learned to laugh together at incidents like the old lady who stole the cakes in her umbrella and the one who collected hymn books from all the churches. God's funny people, Frank called them, but there was no laughter the night three youths knocked on our door looking for accommodation.

'We've been on a cycling tour but the weather has been so bad we've given up and want to take the train home to Dunedin. We've run out of money. Can you help us with accommodation and train fares?' I figured they looked decent enough.

'Well I guess you can camp in the garden shed for the night.' They certainly were not getting in the house. 'And, yes, we can give you enough money for the train journey.' At least I hoped we could. That depended on my brand new husband. When Frank knew what I'd done his eyes flashed fire.

'You shouldn't have done that. You don't know who they are.' Mistake number one. I felt like pushing the table against the door in case they crept in during the night. Next morning they washed under the garden tap but we brought them in for breakfast, gave them the money they needed and forgot about them until we received the money back with a letter of thanks for our kindness. What kindness? Letting them sleep in the shed and wash in cold water? I felt a smug look cross my face. Perhaps I was the best judge of character after all but wisdom said don't comment so I didn't. I was learning fast.

It seemed that Frank relied heavily on me in those days of ministry. It wasn't difficult to take the lead in the light of his inadequacies. I'd had to manage the financial affairs when he was sick, and he was content to let me continue. In fact it still continues in spite of theories put forward by some marriage counsellors – that a woman handling the money will bring disaster in a marriage.

It's never been a problem in our relationship. Sometimes I have been reluctant to spend money on myself because of my responsibility but that was what I chose. Surely there is no fixed rule. Rather two mature people working a system which suits them best. Two babies made it impossible to share the ministry as we had been doing. My support became more in the background except on occasions such as in one spring flower service when Frank fainted as he was about to preach.

Two men took him out and I picked up his Bible, turning to the text I knew he'd chosen for his sermon. 'Consider the lilies of the field.' If he had left his notes it would have been useful. The Holy Spirit was adequate but why did the deaf man take his hearing aid out when I preached? How I thanked God for the Army's requirement that officers' wives must also go through Bible college training.

We've discovered so many ministers' wives feel inadequate to meet the challenges of the ministry, but not me. Experience made all the difference. Frank learned early to be wary of possible compromising situations. He'd been delivering *War Crys*, the Salvation Army's publication.

'I'll not go to Mrs Berry's again,' he told me. 'You can go in future.' I sensed his agitation. 'That woman tried to seduce me.'

'Surely not Frank, she wouldn't do that.'

'She did and I'm not going back.' It became my lot to take the paper to her. We remembered an officer who had been accused of committing adultery with a woman he had driven home in his car. It was his word against hers. The Salvation Army had no choice but to remove him from office.

His innocence was established five years later when the woman confessed as she lay dying that she had lied about the whole episode. Five wasted years of pew sitting. Of course the Army reinstated him, but Frank became cautious in his dealings with women. He didn't want any lost years.

Often he's asked his secretary to be present during counselling sessions or he'll leave the door of his office open. Women were not welcome in his car if he was alone.

'Beward of compromising situations,' he warns

aspirants to the ministry. 'One false move and your credibility can be lost.' I've never doubted Frank's fidelity nor had any reason to be jealous.

'You have a lovely husband,' one of our old ladies often told me. I agreed. I also developed a sixth sense about men. It was difficult to reconcile the behaviour of some people professing to love God but denying the standards of the Bible. In all his travelling when Frank experienced tremendous loneliness he'd write a letter home. A mutual trust developed which has never waned.

But Christians are human beings. Sometimes extremely unreasonable. Would we ever learn to live with congregations who placed impractical demands on our time? There were women's meetings, missionary meetings, visitation and a home to keep. It seemed I could go a week with everything neat and in order but if one morning the dishes were still in the sink at 10 a.m. someone would always call.

My own skills and gifts were lost in a quagmire of congregational expectations. I struggled to keep my head above the mire especially following our Pentecostal experience.

Those Pentecostals expected me to overflow with spiritual gifts and once rejoiced that I had brought a prophetic message when all I'd done was read two verses from Isaiah. If Frank was caught reading he was lazy. If the children said a word in church they were undisciplined. I prickled all over.

'Now, now, cool down. What they say doesn't matter.' Frank was right. I admired his self-control. Then I decided I wasn't answerable to the congregation but to Frank – and God. Nor was he answerable to them. He once told a difficult deacon that neither he nor the church employed us. God did.

There were other pressures in the Assemblies of God. Now I was expected to prepare the communion and attend to baptismal gowns. It took us a long time to realise that some other ladies in the congregation would love to share the duties long considered the responsibility of the pastor's wife and in doing so developed their own gifts. Frank's ministry developed so fast that I found it difficult to keep up with him but I figured if I cooked him good meals and kept his shirts ironed I'd be doing just fine.

'Thanks, dear, that was a good meal,' he'd often say after dinner. But then, unlike some pastors we knew, he was always home on time to eat it. My respect for this fiery, half Irishman of mine grew as his ministry developed under the good hand of God.

I'd listen to him counselling and wonder where he found the wisdom he was sharing until I remembered God had said, 'If any of you lack wisdom let him ask of God that giveth to all men liberally . . . and it shall be given to him' (James 1:5).

Not only did he know how to handle people in his congregation but also his 'dragging behind' wife once we learned not to argue. A pity. I loved an argument. But then I could turn it into a full-scale war where as Frank was a peaceable man. The odd thing was that we really felt the same about the topic in question. We simply came at it from different angles. Besides, arguing didn't advance the ministry and I knew I must let nothing damage that.

I have never understood why he'd dodge a pothole in the road by swinging the car wide toward oncoming traffic while I crept closer to the curb. Mind you I may not be much of a driver, for if Frank was travelling in the car with me I never got my hands on the wheel. Secretly I suspect that he has something against women drivers.

If a motorist wouldn't let him change lanes he'd say, 'I'll bet it's a woman driver.' I feel so smug if it happens to be a man. But one day I went too far. We were driving across Sydney's harbour bridge on our way to the office when a woman driver attempted to make a dangerous manoeuvre to get in front of us. I knew it was dangerous but I did not approve of the way Frank slowed down in protest.

I put my hand on his knee as I quoted last Sunday's text: 'Blessed are the meek.' He exploded. 'Mind your own business.' I burst into tears.

'Let me out of the car. I'll walk.' This would have been difficult seeing there were three lanes of fast-moving cars between me and the footpath. The silence was ominous. Suddenly the space between us seemed to have stretched to three feet.

When we finally drove into a quiet side street he pulled in to the curb, took me in his arms, kissed me and said, 'I'm sorry.' Anyone would have thought that I'd have known better than to preach at the man after living with him for thirty-seven years.

The story made a great illustration in future sermons. Mind you I often find myself mentioned in sermons.

'My wife is one in a million. To look at her you'd think she was won in a raffle,' he has often said when in full-flight preaching. Suddenly every head in the congregation turns in my direction to see my reaction as they laugh uproariously. I smile sweetly, looking straight at the pulpit. Again he'll say, 'You know that he that getteth a wife getteth a good thing,' with emphasis on thing.

'Do you ever get embarrassed when Frank talks about you like that?' people ask. 'No. Why should I? I know his heart and his love of the dramatic.' Well perhaps I did a little at first.

Now I say that if he didn't have me he wouldn't have any illustrations. Mind you it is amazing what can creep into sermons.

'You people who eat white sugar. It's the white death. If you measured into a cup the amount of sugar you put in your tea and sprinkle on your food in one day you'd be amazed at how much you use.' I saw a young man give up sugar altogether after Frank did that to him. The cup was three quarters full. 'That's beside what you cook in food and the natural sugars you eat,' he pointed out. I've often wondered what the doctors in the congregation think of these impromptu health talks and what does it have to do with the gospel.

'You can serve God better with a strong body. Anyway who wants to be sick? Sick people die and I don't want to go to Heaven yet. There's too much to be done.' So one shelf of the kitchen cupboard groans under the weight of bottles of vitamin capsules and garlic tablets. Doctors' objections are dismissed as a matter of course. I took to reading labels when grocery shopping, learned to cook without capsicums (peppers), mushrooms and tomatoes and to eat chocolate secretly.

'Whose god is their belly and whose end is destruction,' Frank would quote again and again.

'Are you difficult to live with?' he asked me quite unexpectedly one day when he was reading a book on health.

'I don't know. Am I? You had better answer that one. You live with me,' I parried.

'I'm not committing myself but if you are you might need to increase your intake of calcium.' I let the matter drop. But sermons are more than health talks. Unless they resulted in decisions for Christ Frank would come home from church low in spirit and weary in body.

'It wasn't a very good day today. Only one answered the call for people to come to Jesus.'

'How can you measure what was achieved?' I'd ask. Time often revealed that much was accomplished in someone's life in such meetings. The problem was mainly physical exhaustion.

'I guess it's like Jesus when he felt virtue go out of him,' Frank often says.' I can never understand why people come for prayer when the meeting's finished and I'm exhausted. They want their own private altar

147

call I think.' Nevertheless there are occasions when he asks the deacons to bring someone to his office where he can minister to them while I pace up and down almost asleep on my feet.

'I'll never marry a pastor again,' I mutter.

'It must be wonderful living with such a lovely man,' a woman said. She was judging the preacher who jumps up and down on the platform, stalks up the aisle, falls on his knees to illustrate a point and waggles his left leg in an action others try to imitate but can't.

Maybe she had been one of those dampened by Frank's drinking water flung across the congregation in the enthusiasm of a high point. Once the people thought it was the Latter Rain falling.

'He's not like that at home,' I assured her. 'He is a quiet person really.' Her look suggested I was lying. Why do people put pastors on pedestals? I live with him. I should know. She might have thought differently had she known his attitude to my snoring. It was 2 a.m. when his patience failed. A sharp poke in the ribs and I was wide awake.

'Stop that snoring. I haven't had any sleep,' he grumbled.

'Lovely man indeed,' I muttered angrily as I grabbed a spare blanket and marched into the lounge to finish the night in peace. Morning brought sanity and forgiveness. God did say, forget those things which are behind. We did – until the next time I snored. I still take his cup of tea to him before he climbs out of bed. None of these things are major disasters. Instead they give life a touch of humour, that is if our humour is operating, and it keeps us from getting too much into the heavenlies.

No, the drama usually occurred in the counselling room. Although we share most things Frank never breaks confidences by telling me what people say in private. I never expect him to. That was why I was surprised the night he sank into an easy chair, a troubled look on his face.

'I've had a horrible experience today. I've got to get if off my chest,' he told me. He had my full attention.

'What's happened?'

'A young fellow who just became a Christian felt he had to confess to a terrible incident in his life before he could find peace. He felt God couldn't forgive him.'

'Sure you want to tell me about it?' I didn't want Frank to tell me something he would regret.

'Yes I do. For days this man watched a twelve-year-old boy walking along a track between his home and nearby shops. One evening, apparently driven by a terrible passion, he violently assaulted the boy leaving him so shocked by the experience he lay numb and speechless as his attacker walked away. I can't get that twelve-year-old out of my mind.'

Words were useless. I could only hold him tight, respecting as I did his confidence and the fact he never mentioned names. God would have to handle this one. Pain which touches one touches the other as did our grief when we suffered the loss of the parents who had provided secure homes and heaps of love. Frank's mother died while we drove to her bedside. The agony of loss tore at Frank's heart as he knelt by the bed on which her body lay. Great sobs shook him. My thoughts ran to our wedding day.

'Hazel, remember Frank will always be my son,' that little lady reminded me.

'Yes Mum, I'll remember,' I assured her.

I felt this kind of sorrow could only be relieved by tears. I let him cry as I stood with my hand on his shoulder. I didn't want him to be like some who stand dry-eyed at a graveside without having wept in private. Nor did I want the pressure of well-meaning Christians who would say people were brave because they didn't cry. We did cry. Four times as our parents went into the presence of God. Suddenly we realised we were the older generation. There was strength and comfort in each other's love.

No cliches from someone telling us all things work together for good. We knew that without being told. Hadn't that Scripture kept us trusting God through pain we found almost impossible to bear. Fortunately most of our congregation gave us the support we needed, especially in the days of Frank's extended travelling. These long separations were not easily handled. Letters were inadequate when he longed for adult conversation. Sometimes they didn't even arrive. The children missed Daddy.

I found it wasn't easy being mother and father to five lively youngsters and then having to remember I was only mother when he came home. But following Daddy's movements on a world map on the wall helped. This way I hoped the children would feel part of the ministry as we prayed for Daddy and that our sacrifice was an offering to God.

Twenty years down the road Frank wonders if he should have travelled so much when the children were small.

He was constantly thinking of their spiritual welfare and writing letters of concern.

Dearest Hazel and kids,

I really love it here in Fiji. The hunger in the hearts of the people everywhere is terrific. Our church must ever have a burden for unreached souls.

If they haven't got the vision yet then we must see they get it. I could not wish nor pray for more than that we as a family, from Maureen down to Judith and we two, could become a great soul-winning team for Jesus. This will be if we put our hearts and minds to the task.

Another time he wrote from overseas he mentioned especially the two boys, now high school age.

I have had Brian and Graeme very much on my heart these last few days. I have been especially praying that God will help them to stand for Christ at school especially against all the filthy stories and evil talk by boys whose minds are cesspools of filth.

There is a great secret to life if you know how to keep your mind off evil things. 'Thou wilt keep him in perfect peace whose mind is stayed on thee' is a very precious Bible promise. God bless you boys. I have faith in you and believe you will follow Jesus and not the ungodly crowd going down to hell.'

'How do you cope with Frank's absences?' folk ask.

'By developing my own interests and keeping involved in ministry,' is my reply. Any other reaction is a waste of time. The only month I fretted over his absence was the one he spent at Oral Roberts' ministers' seminar in Tulsa, Oklahoma. That time I allowed anger to eat into me because wives were not included.

'Wives ought to be included,' I told everybody who would listen. Few did. 'Come on woman, get yourself together. You're not there so make the most of being at home.' I knew I could choose to be miserable or I could choose to be happy. Being happy seemed the most sensible. I never allowed myself to get angry like that again. My problem was to keep independence in its proper place.

'Is your wife coming?' pastors would ask when Frank accepted an invitation to preach.

'Will they pay my fare?' I'd ask, maintaining if they really wanted me they would do that.

'We don't have the money to pay for her,' they said.

'Neither do we.' End of conversation as we were once more condemned to time apart.

'I wish you were coming,' Frank would say and I would wish I was if only to combat the overwhelming loneliness Frank feels when away from home.

'Ours is a happy marriage. We're never together to fight,' I'd joke with a trace of cynicism.

There was always someone else besides the family at the airport to meet him. Sometimes a crowd of others.

'Why do they all need to come? Don't they realise we want to be alone?'

'They are also pleased to see me back,' was all he'd say.

I stopped objecting when I realised how much it meant to Frank to know his people cared. Not only did people come to the airport but the telephone would butt in on our privacy. Sometimes the telephone seemed to govern our lives, intruding into family life and interrupting meals.

'Let it ring,' I'd say.

'No. You never know who is on the other end. It might be an emergency.' He was right of course. Middle of the night calls were always the worst. To be awakened out of a sound sleep at 2.30 a.m. never helped me be my best and Frank never heard the ringing. I learned to sift calls after Doug rang at 2 a.m.

'Pastor, I am just ringing to tell you that the prophecy you prophesied four years ago has come to pass.'

'What did I prophesy?'

'You said that if I didn't give up alcohol I'd lose my wife and my business. Well I have.'

'And you rang at 2 a.m. to tell me that. Well if you don't hang up I'll prophesy again.' Frank was annoyed. He'd have trouble going back to sleep.

I learned to distinguish calls. 'How long have you had the problem?' I'd ask.

'Six months.'

'Then it will keep till morning.'

'Thanks dear,' a sleepy voice would mutter. But I knew the anguish in Bill's voice as he pleaded for Frank to rescue him from the forces driving him to suicide.

'Here Frank, you had better take this call.'

'Where are you Bill? Don't do anything silly. I'll be there as soon as I can.' Frank climbed out of bed without a murmur. Any life and death occasion was a legitimate interruption to sleep. As soon as he left to rescue Bill I made up a bed ready for their return. I knew that Bill would spend the rest of the night with us. Perhaps more than that. Times like this the rule of keeping problems out of the house were broken.

Then there was the night Bryan Blake rang. It was another 2 a.m. call. I recognised his voice as soon as he spoke. What does he want this time? I lay back on my pillow as he rambled on with his promises to give the church a million dollars as soon as his latest scheme paid off. He's off on another delusion I concluded. I let him ramble, the receiver lying on the pillow beside my ear.

Frank said he kept telling me to hang up. I didn't hear him. The next I knew it was 4 a.m. Bryan was in the middle of saying he must hang up now.

'Thanks for listening Mrs Houston.' I mumbled something about it being just fine as the phone clicked off. 'You should have hung up,' Frank said once more.

'I couldn't. I've been asleep for two hours and didn't hear a thing.' Next day Bryan sent me a large box of chocolates with a card of thanks. 'Dear Lord, don't let him ever find out I didn't hear a word.'

While the children collected lame animals Frank collected lame people, wounded in spirit and starved of love and understanding.

'I think Lester is having a nervous breakdown. Can we have him to stay a few days?'

'Do we really have to have him stay in the house. I'll have to put a mattress down on the floor.' I wasn't always willing for the inconvenience. Frank's positive attitude sometimes irked me but anything was better than the negativity of this boy. It took four days of concentrated ministry before he could see the love and the grace of God toward the repentant soul.

'Replace your negative thoughts with positive ones,'

Frank would tell him. That discipline was too difficult for Lester to maintain. He dropped out of church. 'Lord, You'll have to deal with him. I've done all I know.' Frank would tell me that you can't help people who will not help themselves. Neither could he dismiss them from his mind. I knew what he was thinking. After thirty-nine years of marriage we knew each other's thoughts.

There is more than a little balding round the temples now. In fact Frank is getting quite thin on top. Once, years before, he decided a hairpiece would cover the thinning patch. How was it possible he could wear it for a week and I not notice. A hairpiece proved a nuisance.

A better way would be to ask the Lord to do something about it. Placing his hand on his head he shouted, 'Lord, this has gone far enough.' It was another fifteen years before I noticed it had receded further and silver lines tinted the brown. He is also finding greater difficulty combing his hair over that patch on top.

One evening as we sat quietly, him reading, me writing, I popped a question at him. 'Frank, how many books have you read on marriage?'

'None. Perhaps I did read one. Why?'

'Well I've never read any. Do you think that is why we have had a successful marriage? We never knew ahead of time what problems could arise so we never anticipated any.'

'Maybe,' he grunted as he went back to his book. Can any marriage be perfect? But I was glad he was there.

Chapter 12

A QUIVER FULL

Frank stood by the bassinet gazing at the seven-and-a-half pound 'should have been a boy' scrap of humanity. The fact that this child was part of himself – and me – filled him with awe. The plans we made. She would be a woman of God. Any child of ours would naturally be pliable as we moulded her for the life we wanted her to live. She'd do all the things we had not been able to achieve in our childhood. We dreamed on.

It was something of a shock to realise she was born with a mind of her own. Didn't she know four-hourly feeds were sufficient for a baby her size and that she shouldn't cry half the night, keeping her father awake when he needed his sleep to combat that 'tight band' slowly getting tighter round his head. Three weeks after Maureen's birth he went to hospital. Perhaps the baby sensed more of the tension of those days than we realised. No doubt my own tensions contributed to her fretfulness.

None of the other four was as difficult in their early days but they also had minds of their own. How could five children in the same family be so different? We quickly discovered they each had to be treated as the individuals they are. Gifts from God we called them. Did God really send such mischievous gifts?

'What's in them is also in you,' a frequent visitor would tell us when we reprimanded them in his presence. Was he saying that we were also imperfect?

Well perhaps church would make them perfect. From the first Sunday they were home the babies went to church. We went well-armed with toys: the silent kind. Enough so that when the child lost interest in one it could be replaced with another. Father couldn't tolerate noisy toys even as he frowned on biscuits and cordials in church.

The children learned to sleep wrapped in blankets on the floor. I envied mothers who could sit with husbands in church. The measure of grace I needed to control the children on my own always seemed to be in short supply. We didn't count on bringing up the children in the full glare of congregations who seemed to know better than we did how to raise children. Those PKs. A deacon in one church always referred to our children that way. Pastor's kids indeed.

'Don't you single our children out like that,' I responded angrily.

'My children are no different from yours. They have the same aptitude for mischief and the same possibilities for God.' I wanted to add 'so there' but Frank would never have approved. Years later I would probably have told them in a nice kind of way to mind their own business. Frank supported my point of view. We'd support each other even if we didn't agree one hundred per cent.

I'm not sure what Dr Spock would have said. He was the only 'authority' anyone read in the early fifties and he bred generations of undisciplined children in spite of his good points. Dr Dobson wasn't around. We only had the Bible. 'Bring up a child in the way he should go and when he is old he will not depart from it.' We clung to that and are still clinging to it.

We did get one piece of advice. It came in a letter of congratulation from a grandfather. 'Having had the joy of watching two little lives come into our home and develop and grow into manhood we can understand your happiness ... with the joy comes the responsibility to set before this little one from the

156

earliest beginnings that pattern of life and example that will lead her feet early into Christian values.

'The regularity of the family altar observance, the teaching of the little one a baby's lisped prayer with her earliest ability to speak and your vital efforts for the building of the kingdom of God before her will contribute to her proper upbringing for future usefulness to God.'

Frank introduced the family altar. More accurately he inflicted the family altar, adult-style, on the kids. Frank read the Bible, King James version, asked a few questions about the reading and prayed. Kids wriggled and I missed what he said trying to keep them quiet. At amen they bolted out the door to resume the game Dad had interrupted.

As the children grew older Father thought of a new trick for Sunday lunch times.

'Can anyone tell me what my text was this morning?' he asked. They stared in silence.

'So you weren't listening today,' he reprimanded them. The kids were quick to catch on. Next time he asked they knew his text. What he'd said about it was another matter. Brian looked guilty remembering that Father had marched down to him when people had their eyes closed to reprimand him for misbehaviour. With a clip on the ear and a warning, 'You sit there and behave or else,' he marched back to the platform.

Some teaching did sink in although it did not always have the desired effect. The topic under discussion was the second coming of Jesus.

'Yes, one day Jesus will catch us up into the air and take us into Heaven,' the lesson concluded.

'But I don't want to go up into the air,' ten-year-old Brian wailed.

'Why ever not?'

'Because my trousers might fall off,' he sobbed. 'Besides, I don't want Him to come until I get married and have children.'

We didn't bargain on the lessons the children would teach us. Like the morning Frank was out digging the garden.

Graeme had decided to stay in bed that morning with a severe headache and an ugly lump in his groin. Suddenly the bedroom window opened and a little head popped out.

'Daddy, will you come and pray for me?' Graeme asked.

'Sure son. I'll just finish this job and I'll be right in.' Frank went on digging forgetting the request in his efforts to finish the job. Half an hour later the window banged open again.

'Daddy, I got sick of waiting for you so I prayed for myself.'

'What happened?'

'I got healed of course.'

God gave us other miracles. He healed Brian of hepatitis, diagnosed by one doctor and declared a mistaken diagnosis by another as he did not believe hepatitis could disappear so quickly.

The most dramatic healing happened the night I found Brian choking. He had been perfectly well when he went to bed an hour before I went into the room to put some clothes away. A strange gurgle coming from the top bunk caught my attention. At a glance I could see Brian's face was blue and he was struggling to breathe. I dropped the clothes in a heap on the floor, dragged the boy over the edge of the bunk crying out 'In the name of Jesus.' He'd been sick all over himself and was unconscious but his colour began to improve.

'Lord, what shall I do first?' I cried.

I knew we needed the doctor and Brian needed a bath but I was afraid to lay him down for a single moment. 'Please Lord, send Frank home from the youth meeting. I need him.'

Frank, by now halfway through his message to the

youth, suddenly began to lose his train of thought. As he fumbled for the right words he decided to finish.

'I'm going home. You carry on,' he told the youth leader.

As Frank walked in the door I thrust Brian into his arms. 'He's sick. I must call the doctor.' Frank prayed. I made the call. Anxiously we waited for the doctor's verdict.

'I can't decide if he had a convulsion because he was sick or if he was sick because he'd had a convulsion. It could be he had a fit.' The doctor administered an injection.

'That will relax him but I think I should put him in hospital. He needs continual watching.'

'Can't we keep him home, doctor.' Frank knew there was no faith in a hospital while at home there was. The doctor hesitated.

'Well if you watch him constantly all night, take his pulse at midnight and phone me, then perhaps you can.'

Frank determined that he would watch the child so he could pray in tongues until night dragged into morning.

'You get some sleep,' he told me, knowing my difficulty in coping with sleeplessness. At midnight Brian's pulse was still erratic. The doctor dropped in again obviously worried that there appeared to be no change in Brian's condition. At 6 am, as we sipped an early cup of tea, a small boy opened his eyes, looked up at his father and said, 'Hullo Dad. I'm hungry,' and went in search of the box of Weetbix.

There was yet a great deal of living and learning to do for all of us, as we discovered the day we found Brian sitting in a police car. We had been to a picnic with the Bible college students. Frank walked over to the car.

'Well young man, what have you been up to?'

'I rode Jim Shelling's motorbike.'

'But you can't ride a motorbike.'

'Graeme showed me how,' the boy sobbed.

'He didn't show you how to stop,' the policeman said gruffly. He looked at Graeme.

'Are you sure you didn't ride the bike as well?' Brian jumped to Graeme's defence. 'He didn't ride it. Only I did.' He wouldn't change his story though we were all suspicious.

'The owner will need to come to the station to make a statement and tell us if he wishes to lay charges. In the meantime we'll leave the boy with you.' The policeman climbed back into his car and drove off.

'Right,' said Father. 'You had better tell me exactly what happened. Are you sure Graeme didn't ride it?'

'No, only me,' Brian sobbed. 'I rode it up the road but when the police car came up to the corner I didn't know how to stop so I just fell off in front of them.' The agony of a suppressed grin crossed Frank's face.

'Don't you realise you could have been killed? Don't you ever do that again,' he said, and, turning to Graeme, 'Or you.' But three days later the bike had been moved again.

'Have you two boys had that motorbike again?' Frank was angry. Brian looked to Graeme for help.

'I cannot tell a lie. It was Brian,' Graeme hastily said.

'It was not.' Brian was indignant. 'Graeme is lying.' Or was it Brian? Careful sifting of the facts revealed Graeme was the culprit. But that wasn't the only time Frank had to sift through a story. Beverley and Brian came in after school one day with pockets full of coins.

'Look what we found,' they burst out.

'Where did you get it from?' Frank asked. 'We found it under the hedge in the park.' A likely tale. Fear that they had stolen the money was foremost in our minds.

'Now I want the truth,' Frank stressed. 'Where did you get it?'

'We did find it in the park,' they claimed in duet.

'If you don't tell me the truth I will get the strap to you.' Frank was getting exasperated. The children stuck with their story. Father kept his word.

Two howling children still insisted they had told the truth. We discovered later it was the truth. That day we learned that impossible stories might just happen to be true. How can you withdraw an unjust punishment? I consoled them with the thought that this spanking would serve for all the ones they should have had for misdemeanours we hadn't discovered. Years later when the family was together talking about childhood escapades we discovered there were quite a few. And we thought we knew everything. It was in 1966 that the Beatles came to town.

'Those fellows with the weird hairdos will be a bad influence on our young people,' Frank concluded. The Sunday they were to arrive Frank issued a warning to the youth in the morning service.

'I trust none of you will go to meet the Beatles at the airport. It isn't any place for Christians.' Service over Beverley pressured her father into letting her go into the city to a friend's for lunch. It just so happened they could see the planes landing from Janet's house nestling on the hillside. Lunch over the two girls went for a walk – right down to the airport. A policeman, seeing two small girls by a hole in the fence, thought they might get crushed by the swarming crowd of teenagers behind them.

'Come through and stay by me,' he said, helping them through the hole in full view of the media. Television cameras zoomed in on them.

Newspaper and radio journalists interviewed them.
'What is your name?'
'Beverley Houston.'
'How old are you?'
'Ten.'
'Where do you live?'
'In Lower Hutt.' When the policeman moved across

to the plane when it landed the two girls stayed with him as he'd said. The whole world knew that the pastor's daughter had actually met the Beatles. 'That'll give the congregation something to talk about,' I muttered.

Frank laughed. Some would say that was the beginning of rebellion but she hadn't been specifically told not to go. Beverley learned we loved her and understood something of the thinking of a ten-year-old. No it wasn't that which caused rebellion. Rather it was a loosening of her grip on God and confusion when a guest preacher spoke on deliverance with long deliverance sessions following. We didn't realise how some of the scenes had affected her at the time. As a teenager and beyond she shuddered at the thought of it. If only she had seen the Deliverer instead of deliverance. But 'if onlys' are a waste of time.

It was Beverley who would challenge us about which church she should attend. It seemed to be the natural course for the children to stay in the Assemblies of God. Beverley at sixteen would make us rethink our position.

'You wouldn't like it if I went to another church,' she challenged us in a fit of rebellion.

'We don't mind which one you go to as long as it is evangelical and doctrinally sound,' Frank told her. Determined to test Frank's sincerity she went off to the Salvation Army the next Sunday night.

'Well, how did you enjoy it?' Frank asked.

'Dad you wouldn't believe it. Captain Padman recognised me and publicly welcomed me.' She looked embarrassed even as she told us. Ah well, experience shoots the lesson home. Still, her church attendance became spasmodic, but when she did come there was always a wave for her father from the back of the church and a surreptitious scratching of the ear as Father acknowledged her arrival from the platform. Beverley and her father had a perfect understanding.

Graeme also determined to show his independence by moving into a flat with some friends. Hair over his shoulders and wearing raggedy jeans he could listen to all the rock music he wanted to without me praying for the Lord to stop it. I don't think he ever found out why the record player suddenly refused to go.

His lifestyle worried us when we remembered the world of drugs and sex. Yet this was the son who, some years later, would hitch-hike six hundred miles from Brisbane to Sydney to meet us at the airport when we came to preach at a camp. Our host scowled at Graeme's appearance but we accepted him as he was. 'We must always keep the door of communication open so that he can come home when he wants to. If we cut off communication we will never be able to help him,' Frank said. I agreed. Frank arrived home from a meeting one night to find a note from Graeme on the kitchen bench.

'Dad, please wake me up, I want to talk to you.' He'd decided to sleep at home that night. No, I still do not know what they talked about but there was satisfaction in knowing that Graeme felt free to come to his father.

God challenged my attitudes towards this long-haired son. I was preparing to speak to the youth group at a fancy dress night they were having. My choice of verse was appropriate. 'For the Lord seeth not as man seeth: man looketh on the outward appearance but the Lord looketh on the heart' (1 Sam. 16:7).

'Those young people are not as they appear,' I wrote.

'Neither is Graeme.' It was like the still small voice mentioned in the Scripture. The realisation shook me as I remembered the Christmas he and his girlfriend, Carolyn, and a friend made sandwiches which they took to the alcoholics in the city parks.

'As much as ye have done it unto one of the least of these my brethren ye have done it unto me,' Jesus said.

Graeme followed from afar. No devious scheming of ours would reach him but God had His own way.

He eventually joined the fire brigade and as part of his training he watched a post-mortem on a twenty-year-old boy, the victim of a car accident.

'If that were me I wouldn't go to Heaven,' Graeme confessed to himself. 'I'd be in hell.' He plunged into deep depression, crying for weeks. Neither his wife nor long-distance phone calls from his father could lift him out of it. Frank caught a plane for New Zealand. Even a visit from his father wasn't the answer. How we prayed that God would heal him. A feeling possessed him that he might die himself before too long. Worry upon worry deepened the stress of sleepless nights. As Graeme lay tossing in the darkness he thought of the Bible Frank had given him for his eighteenth birthday. Perhaps it might have something to help him. In the early hours of the morning he rummaged in the cupboard until he'd found it. He wondered what he should read. As he turned the front cover he noticed the Scripture reference his dad had written on the flyleaf ten years before. Proverbs 3 – he'd read that.

'My son, forget not My law but let thine heart keep My commandments. For length of days, and long life, and peace shall they add to thee.' God began to speak gently to a son who dwelt in darkness. Graeme read on. From the promise of life in verse 2 through to verse 24 which told him that 'when he lay down his sleep would be sweet', every distressing worry was answered in that chapter.

This was the turning point. Finally Carolyn's comforting love helped Graeme back to health as the depression slowly lifted.

He and Carolyn began to come back to church until a woman verbally attacked Graeme over certain actions.

'You shouldn't be doing that. You're Pastor Houston's

son,' she told him. The two young people walked off hurt and embarrassed.

'How can people be so insensitive? Why don't they leave the Holy Spirit to do His own work,' Frank cried.

'Unfortunately God's people are often insensitive. The Holy Spirit doesn't need our help to convict sinners and I am not sure why we think He does,' I replied thoughtfully.

That God is more merciful than people was proved in the experience which almost shattered our world. We were sitting comfortably by the fire one night when our daughter and her boyfriend came in.

'Do you want a cup of coffee?' I asked.

'Sit down Mum, I've got something to tell you.' Her voice contained an unusual gravity. There was a long pause then she continued, 'I'm pregnant.'

For a moment we had no reaction. Then deep unreasonable anger swept through me as I realised the implications. Fingers would be pointed at us and we would have to resign from the ministry. Twenty years ago a pre-marital pregnancy in any circle was regarded as the ultimate disgrace.

There would be some ready to accuse the pastor of this inability to control his children.

'You'd better leave,' I told the boy.

'Don't be so hasty,' Frank reprimanded me.

'I'll have the baby adopted,' our daughter volunteered.

'I'll pay for her to go to Australia,' her boyfriend offered.

After they had left we discussed the situation. Should we tell the church and the other children or just Trevor Chandler. As our associate pastor he should know. We didn't tell anyone but we should have done. Someone else eventually told the children.

'We will have to resign from the church,' Frank said.

A day later when the heat of the moment had passed I began to ask myself had God removed the call to the ministry at this time or was this an attack of the devil designed to smash our ministry. We fell on our knees before God. I voiced my thoughts to Frank.

'I don't think we should resign. God hasn't lifted the call.' He agreed.

Our daughter went to Australia but a noted trouble-maker in the church asked the people at the next prayer meeting to pray for the Houston's family situation.

Did she suspect something and was spreading gossip in a spiritual guise? We never found out.

Our hearts continued to ache and our daughter suffered extreme homesickness as she sheltered in a Salvation Army home from a hostile world. We decided she must come home.

We arranged for her to go as companion to an elderly lady over the mountains from our valley. Within us there was a monumental struggle between the desire to keep the baby and face the consequences or proceed with the adoption.

'Frank, I think we should keep the baby. It might be another statistic to the Government but it is our grandchild and I want it. I can look after it.'

'I've been thinking the same thing,' he said. We hurried over the mountains to tell our daughter what we had decided.

That day we saw a light in our daughter's eyes which had been missing for a long time and God removed the ache in our hearts. But people are not so forgiving. Months after the baby was born, some by their attitude screamed condemnation at the young mother until an agonised cry fell from her lips.

'Mum, when does God forgive?'

'As soon as we confess our sin from a repentant heart.'

'Then why don't people also forgive us?' Why indeed.

'Unfortunately people are not like God.' Frank and I both would have carried her pain but she had to work through it herself. 'Do you realise the times I longed to sit on your bed and talk after an evening out?' she asked one day years after she was married. No I hadn't realised.

Was it easier to understand the needs of a procession of sick animals and birds which found their way to our door – usually in Beverley's arms? That grubby little pigeon half dead with lice. I knew how to treat lice. They'd succumb to doses of poultry lice powder.

Frank didn't understand about animals but he did understand people. It was too difficult for me to stay awake until the children were in at night to have a conference but Frank always knew when they arrived home. Bringing up the children was an adventure in laughter as well as tears.

From pacing the football field encouraging our young sons' play even when one raced away from the other players to score a grand try – albeit at the wrong goal line – to enjoying Judith's teen years there has been lots of laughter:

Judith, the one I thought I was too old to have, has probably been the easiest to handle. The only child born after we were filled with the Holy Spirit.

'Are you saying I was a mistake, Mum?' she asks with a twinkle in her eyes.

'No, not a mistake, a surprise. But a jolly good one.' Not that she was perfect. Oh no. This child who told everyone that Daddy delegated babies instead of dedicated them and that he wasn't invaluable instead of available had a vivid imagination.

'Judith tells me that she had a twin brother who was killed in a car accident,' my neighbour informed me one morning.

'The young minx. There isn't one ounce of truth in it.' Ah, imagination, the seat of creativity.

This child should be creative indeed. But they were all good at imagining. Beverley wouldn't own me as Mother before her schoolmates. My hair was too grey for a mother so I became her grandmother. The only consolation in our mischievous gifts from God was the statement made by some unknown person that mischievous kids were intelligent.

Our children should be top of the group. The relationship we had with them was only slightly marred by their embarrassment when schoolmates asked why their father stared out of the kitchen window. How could they know he frequently prayed for the passersby, including them?

Suddenly they were adults turning thoughts toward marriage. Frank prayed much for them, especially those who seemed to be interested in young people we thought were unsuitable friends. But who wants to listen to any advice when the mind is made up. Beverley's husband, brought up a Catholic, couldn't believe we didn't fight.

Maureen's husband chose Bible college although she wanted to avoid the ministry. The reasons for that we would find out ten years later when she and Ian separated.

On hindsight I knew she'd cried for help a number of times but I'm not sure we would have believed her story had she told it to us. If only we'd known. Again the 'if onlys' were futile. Our hearts ached without relief through the anguish of divorce. It was like a death in the family.

'What about the children?' Frank and I both cried. When she spoke of remarriage two years later I had many questions. Would David understand Maureen's emotional needs and could he be a father to the children? He became the husband and father every family needed.

Graeme's wife, as a child, had also been brought up a Catholic. Carolyn had promised God to go to church every day if He would heal her father from a heart attack. Small girl as she was she did as she had promised. Brian, who planned to enter the ministry, had fallen head over heels in love with a girl four hundred miles away so we couldn't form an opinion.

'Lord, let her be suitable for a minister's wife.' She would either make or break his ministry. Bobbie has helped to make it. Judith fell in love with the head deacon's son who had determined when we was twelve that he'd marry her.

Now more than ever they needed our prayers. Frank continues to pray for them every day along with the grandchildren. God must surely answer. We have survived the traumas of child-rearing while the children have survived our inexperience and our mistakes.

Fifteen grandchildren later we realise that we are very much family when they come running to greet us with open arms. Being grandparents is the best ego booster a person can have. We had no books except the Bible to guide us but by example, sometimes imperfectly, we try to portray the love of God.

Frank's philosophy over the years has been to let the children go so that we might keep them. That we are included in the greater family circle would suggest this to be right. The children have possibly paid a price for the work of the Lord. Maureen says the family all give their father to the ministry. So they do. The decisions the pastor makes can alter the whole course of his family's life but finally they, and us, choose our own ways.

'Remember kids, we are free to make our own choices but we are not free to choose the consequences of those choices,' Frank reminds them. The two who chose to help us in another vision certainly saw some consequences for their choice.

Chapter 13

ENLARGE YOUR TENT

Read Isaiah 54. The whole chapter. The impression pierced the summer darkness of that January night, 1977. Frank snuggled into his pillows as he drowsily contemplated all that God had achieved through the last seventeen years of ministry. He was alone in the house when he 'heard' the command to read the Scripture.

'Isaiah 54. I know that chapter well. Why should I read it?' Suddenly Frank realised he couldn't remember a word. What did that Scripture say? He switched on his bedside lamp, turned his Bible to the chapter and began to read.

'Enlarge the place of your tent . . . lengthen your cords and strengthen your stakes for you shall expand on the right and on the left and your descendants will inherit the nations. . . Do not fear for you shall not be put to shame or disgraced. . . No weapon which is formed against you shall prosper and every tongue which rises against you in judgement you shall condemn.'

What are you saying, Lord? Frank was wide awake now. Slowly a panorama of Sydney passed before him. The bridge, the crowds in George Street, the opera house. He saw them all.

'I want you to go to Sydney and start a church.' Sydney! What a wild idea. It can't be the Lord.

'I'm fifty-five, settled in my own home and ministering to a church which loves me. Even that opposing deacon couldn't get the church to vote me out. I'm sure I have a life call to Lower Hutt,' Frank argued with the Lord.

I'd been travelling through the South Island of New Zealand when God spoke but it was no great surprise to me. I'd been feeling for some time that our work in Lower Hutt was completed.

'But Lord, why Sydney?' I wanted to know. 'You know how I hate Sydney. I could live in Melbourne or even Brisbane but Sydney. No, not Sydney.' I remembered that Frank had often come back from a visit to Australia saying he would love to have 'a crack at Sydney'. I never took the suggestion seriously. But now it was serious. 'Well Lord, you will have to give me a miracle so that I can like the place.' The matter was settled. We agreed we had to go to Sydney. The church in Lower Hutt sensed the excitement of God's call.

'We'll support you for a year,' they said. Frank made two decisions. We'd begin with a big crusade and we wouldn't be part of the Assemblies of God because of its lean towards central control. God showed each of us involved that a crusade would be a mistake. That would have alienated us from other churches. Instead we would just slip in quietly and begin in the Eastern Suburbs where there didn't appear to be any Pentecostal churches.

Frank decided to ask a small group of chosen people to help him but none were really musicians. 'Lord, give us great musicians,' Frank prayed. When the news leaked out that Frank Houston was starting a work in the Eastern Suburbs there was consternation in the city. Insecure pastors felt threatened.

'I am not going to take people from other churches,' Frank said. 'I want to reach the lost and there are still plenty of them amongst four million people.'

'You know that all the best people have tried to establish a church in the Eastern Suburbs and failed,' a fellow minister assured Frank.

'Then I have a problem,' Frank told him. 'When I got filled with the Holy Spirit I dropped the word failure out of my vocabulary.' While there were no

Pentecostal churches that side of Sydney, there was Vision Ministries, a Charismatic organisation specialising in conventions and a Bible school headed up by Rev Alan Langstaff. To us that wasn't a church. But Alan wasn't happy that we would be so close to his work until God dealt with him over his attitude. He shared his experience with Frank assuring him of his support. That day the two men became good friends.

The Easter of '77 Frank and I were ministering in Newcastle, one hundred and fifty miles north of Sydney. It was here that I received my miracle. I'd spoken to a combined women's meeting.

At the end I felt to pray for the ladies as a group. As I did so God gave me a spiritual experience so real that I knew these people were my people. There was also born in me a tremendous love for the city of God's calling. Three months later Frank, Judith and I surveyed our parish from the air as we flew into Sydney, this time to stay. What would God do in this city?

We had neither car nor home but this could not dampen our excitement. Maureen and Ian, our daughter and son-in-law, had preceded our arrival by two months. Their task was to find a hall suitable for meetings. There seemed to be none available. By this time Chris and Bev Aiton with baby Jemima and Peter Mitcheson, the other members of the group who had agreed to help us, had also arrived.

Frank decided to advertise a meeting for interested friends to be held in the Aitons' house the first Sunday afternoon. Only our own group of eight adults and five children would meet for communion and a prayer time in the morning. Frank kept glancing from watch to door as time drew near for the afternoon meeting. Nineteen people came to hear him share the vision. We knew two of them.

Henare and Gabriella Gilbert, who rarely read the religious advertisements, did so that week. They'd been in our church in New Zealand eight years before. When Henare said they'd stay with us Frank knew we had our first great musician, for Henare was a professional singer and entertainer.

It was another miracle when we discovered a small hall hidden down a side street. We'd tried to get school halls and searched the telephone book for lists of auditoriums to no avail. This would do but would the Woollahra Council lease it to us? They did – at $25 a Sunday. Christian Life Centre Sydney was under way. The first Sunday in the hall forty people were in the congregation, including another professional singer and guitarist. Our orchestra was growing apace.

Frank was invited to speak to a bunch of hippies, all new Christians. Amongst them was a pianist who'd played in a rock band. On Christmas Day this group of young people appeared in the church. Trevor King, the pianist and a scruffy lad, sat in the congregation for five weeks. He'd need to change a lot before he could be used in the church.

'Lord, send me an outstanding keyboard player,' Frank kept praying. 'What is that in thine hand?' the Lord asked. Frank looked at his hand.

'There is nothing in my hand Lord.'

Three times the Lord asked the question. Three times Frank gave the same reply. He wakened to the fact that the Lord was telling him he had a top keyboard player right there in the congregation. His pride and old concepts were preventing him from using what God had given. Didn't a fellow have to prove himself before he could be used in church? Frank took a calculated risk.

'Trevor, are you going to play tonight?' Frank asked him. I was shocked that Frank would let him play in the church so soon. Why, he wasn't even dressed properly, unless a black sleeveless singlet, jeans cut off above the knees and frayed round the legs and a hole in the seat revealing red underpants was proper dress.

173

When Trevor played I forgot his clothes in the glory of the music. God dealt with his dress code in the weeks that followed and Frank hadn't said a word.

He realised that we would very quickly need some kind of governing body to help and advise in the administration of the church.

'I'll appoint an interim council with the clear understanding that it is a temporary arrangement,' he told me. 'I will not appoint men I do not know into positions of responsibility. It is easier to put men in positions than it is to get them out if they are unsuitable.

'We will need to have mid-week Bible study meetings in our homes. There is nowhere else to have them.' The others agreed. Frank was sure in later years that God was in this for the foundation set in place then has continued throughout the church's history. No other church we knew worked the system then. With the growth of the work, the home fellowships extended, bringing a shortage of leaders.

'Lord, what am I going to do?' Frank asked of God. 'Use what you've got,' the Lord seemed to say.

This made Frank look closer at what he had. Women! That's who he had. He'd use them. At least the church, being new, had no preconceived ideas about women in ministry. This wasn't any problem to Frank with his Salvation Army background. If they had a ministry in this way why shouldn't they use it.

'We must set our philosophy for the church,' Frank told his council. 'Our aim is to reach the people of this city and to go out into other areas. In fact let our motto be "Our city and beyond".'

The church would reach into the city, teaching and making disciples. It would reach out into other parts of the country, indeed into the world, witnessing to lost and unhappy people. Frank always aimed at a balance between the two. Churches which were only evangelistic tended to breed shallowness.

'Miracles will not stop you backsliding,' he stressed. But churches which concentrated on teaching without evangelism often became introverted and stagnant. No growth; no life.

The Lord warned Frank that all who came to us would not stay. Some would try to use us for their own selfish ends. In our first month that happened when a brother brought his dozen people to join us. He left when he realised that he would not be given leadership. His people stayed and we were blamed for taking them. God knew our hearts.

Those who stayed were far more than those who left. The hall was overcrowded within six months. The police had a busy time writing tickets for illegal parking. Pressure from residents who claimed we made too much noise and the council, who recognised the problem was one of growth, forced us to find other premises. Halls were no easier to find than when we first began. Ian had a bright idea. Perhaps we could find a hotel convention room. We did – for nine months when the problems repeated themselves.

Besides, Frank had a feeling that some of the characters starting to come to the meetings were not welcome in the hotel. The search for a hall was fruitless. We tried to lease an old church in the city but when the dozen members discovered we were Pentecostal they closed the doors to us.

Frank and Brian, now on our staff, saw a 'to lease' sign on the wall of a building close to the hotel. An open door encouraged them to investigate the property. On the second floor they found Ian with the real estate agent. The building had been empty for three years but with heaps of paint and elbow grease it could become a suitable home for the church. Frank decided on the spot to take the ground floor subject to council approval for its use as a church. God had said stretch your tent. We were doing that. To thirteen thousand square feet with twenty-four-hour a day access and no rent until the place was ready for occupation in three months' time.

The offices moved to the new building immediately. It wasn't easy working amongst sawdust and hammering as alterations took shape. On Fridays Ian organised the volunteers to clear and sweep the foyer area so that it could become a sanctuary on Sunday.

'Why even the foyer can hold three hundred and fifty people.' Frank was delighted. Volunteers scraped and painted. Sometimes the undercoat went on top of a final coat but it was all part of the fun. Besides their labour, the people gave $45,000 towards the cost of furnishings. Trevor King hovered round the new baby grand piano as though it was part of the crown jewels.

After two years Frank felt it was time to bring the church into the Assemblies of God. He disliked being a 'loner' with its inherent dangers. Already the Commonwealth executive had offered Frank an Assemblies of God ministerial credential on Andrew Evans's recommendation.

'In the light of your standing in New Zealand,' they told him. Frank had accepted the offer. Andrew was releasing the Australian fellowship into freedom similar to that experienced in New Zealand.

'You'll lose the Charismatics if you become Assemblies of God,' some warned. I remembered that we'd often been asked in the beginning were we Charismatic or Pentecostal. 'Call us what you like. I don't know the difference,' I replied. Some thought there was a difference.

'The church will be exactly the same,' Frank reassured them, determined to go ahead with affiliation anyway. There was no difference and nobody left.

They were all too busy reaching our city – the first part of our motto. Frank asked an enthusiastic young man with an evangelistic gift to organise a group he called the 'Christian Commandos'. The invitation to join encouraged participants 'to come prepared to sing, dance, preach and generally proclaim the gospel. Tell Sydney Jesus is alive'.

The first gathering thrilled Frank's evangelistic heart. Girded by two hours of prayer the young people moved onto the streets of Kings Cross, Sydney's notorious red-light area. They decided to stand in a park to witness.

This was homosexual territory. They were pelted with tomatoes and eggs until a twenty-stone Commando marched up to the fellow throwing eggs.

'I advise you to stop,' he told the young fellow as he pushed his big hand hard on the culprit's chest. Scrunch. A dozen eggs still hidden in his shirt became a slippery mess. The police also tried to move them on. The young people would not be moved until they were ready. Then they marched single file through the street down one side and back along the other singing choruses all the way. There were Christians mingling with the crowd waiting to pick up the interested sinners. It wasn't until a local radio station's night patrol interviewed them that they were left in peace.

With growth came other problems. The baptismal services became so frequent that Frank thought it a good idea for the home fellowship leaders to baptise people from their areas. Some immediately asked, 'What about the *women*?'

'*What* about the women?' Frank asked in reply. Silence greeted his question. The women took their turn without further objection. From there to serving at the communion table was a natural evolution. Even William Booth had not gone as far as that for he feared that would divide the movement. But Frank Houston had no such fears. It worked in Christian Life Centre Sydney in 1978. It still does in 1988 and our women are not frustrated.

Our building was filling rapidly as the pastor encouraged the people to bring others with them.

'Church is not about buildings. It's about God and people,' he frequently stressed. 'I hate preaching to empty seats. They cannot respond to altar calls. Bring your friends and neighbours and your families to fill them.'

Yet the multitudes we were not reaching challenged Frank's heart.

'How about some Sunday night concerts in the town hall?' Frank asked Trevor King, now our music minister.

'You can arrange some good items and I'll finish off with a ten minute sermon.'

'The day of miracles is not yet over if you can restrict a sermon to ten minutes,' I said when I heard the plan.

I knew that if I he'd let me edit his sermons he could preach them in half the usual hour, but ten minutes seemed impossible. Frank was nervous as zero hour approached. Could we get a decent crowd in this two thousand-seat auditorium? From a dark corner at the back of the hall Frank kept watch as people flocked in. The ground floor would be full anyway. In the audience was a young man, a member of a very successful rock band. Tired and disillusioned though he was by the rock scene with its drugs and allied lifestyle, he didn't think the Christian world was what he wanted either.

'Why don't you come with me to a Christian concert in the town hall tonight?' his father asked.

'Who wants to go to an amatureish Christian concert?' David replied. But he did come. The choir burst into a lively chorus. A puppet slid down a wire to sit behind the drums as a prelude to the puppet show. Frances Greening, the soloist, soared to the highest note of Sandi Patti's song 'We Shall Behold Him'.

'This is really professional stuff,' David told his father.

At the end of the ten-minute sermon David Moyse walked boldly to the front with other seeking souls.

Trevor King was elated.

'Pastor, did you see who came on the altar call tonight.'

'A number did.'

'Yes but one was David Moyse of the famous group Air Supply.'

'Really.' That information didn't mean much to Frank. David accepted the challenge of Christianity and Christian Life Centre had another top musician. The first part of our motto was being fulfilled but what about the second. Ah, Asia is only eight hours' flying from Sydney.

'Let us go there with the gospel,' Frank said to our missions director. Ian was enthusiastic. A burden for Malaysia sprang up in his heart.

The Ramaya boys, greatly influenced in Frank's meetings years before, were pastoring churches in Malaysia. They would be grateful for some crusades. The young men who went in response to the call opened their hearts to the people.

Unexpected opposition hit their efforts to help the Chinese and Indian nationals. No, not from the Government but the church. Finally our men had to withdraw.

Their crime – preaching in Malaysia without the permission of the Assemblies of God headquarters. No one had thought to let them know of our plans. Frank felt some were kingdom builders but it was their own kingdom. Other countries welcomed our missionaries. Chris and Bev Aiton went off to Manila in the Philippines determined to establish a Christian Life Centre in that city as a springboard into other parts of the country.

Once established, Chris and the Filipinos welcomed our teams of specially chosen people. Three Bible college graduates answered the call to work with the Aitons in church planting. These men would work under Chris's supervision in establishing a new church. Once they had a group meeting together a national pastor would work in the leadership with them. When the church was well established the three Australians would move on to another town. Our vision for the beyond was being fulfilled.

As the church at home grew apace Frank found it necessary to divide the city into regions, each with its own leader. The home fellowships grew beyond the capacity of the area leaders to successfully minister to all the people.

'You fellows will have to accept responsibility as pastors for various areas,' Frank told his men on the staff. Their ministry expanded the home fellowships until eight hundred people were attending each week. Once Frank had Christian Life Centre on the move other churches in the city began to grow. Instead of decreasing as a result of our coming to Sydney they also experienced the moving of God's Spirit. New churches began popping up all over the city. Church growth became fashionable.

Pastors discussed numbers as though they were the all-important factor.

'How many are you getting now?'

'Two thousand.'

'I'm getting two and a half. What about you?' the pastor asked looking at the third.

'I'm averaging about two hundred,' the third replied, embarrassed that his church wasn't bigger.

'How many are you getting now, Frank?' they asked.

'I really don't know. I've told my men they can count the numbers if they want to but they are not to tell me. I'm tired of this numbers game.' He did know there were too many to get into the auditorium in one service.

That made Frank happy for it meant that we were continuing to grow. In spite of the crowds 'Hawke-eye,' as some of his college students in New Zealand had dubbed him, missed people from Sunday services.

'Dick and Loraine haven't been in church for a few weeks', he said to me one Sunday after church. 'I wonder where they are.'

'They're probably on holiday,' I suggested. Frank wasn't satisfied with that explanation. He told the area pastor to find out where they were.

'They are going to another church,' he said. Frank turned their departure over in his mind. 'You know Dick and Loraine have been with us for over seven years. Church growth experts say that after seven years people tend to grow restless and look for another spiritual home. I guess that's what happened to them but I'm sorry. They were amongst the first in Christian Life Centre.'

Again the shepherd heart rued the departure of some of his sheep without even a goodbye.

'You must get to know the people so that you too will know who is missing,' he tells his young ministers.

'When people move to escape their problems they don't realise that their problem is in themselves and they take it with them,' Frank often says.

We lost people for another reason. No, we gave people. It isn't losing to give. It is multiplication by division. It happened this way.

'Dad, I'd like to start a meeting in the Liverpool area. There's nothing happening out there. The local Assemblies of God has only five in it. Would you mind if the people who come into the city from that area helped me?' Our son Brian, now Frank's associate pastor, wanted his father's blessing. Liverpool was an hour's drive from downtown Sydney.

'No, son. If that's what you feel God wants you to do that's fine by me.' The first of our outreach churches was born. That established with its own pastor, Brian commenced a Sunday afternoon meeting in Gosford – a town an hour's drive to the north. This meeting soon developed into a full-scale church. Again another pastor took its leadership. A third followed. In this area we had about forty people who drove for one and a quarter hours into the city every Sunday. As this outreach developed Brian felt he should lead the baby church himself.

'I feel as though my right arm has been cut off,' Frank told me. I knew he was missing the son who was more like a brother in the ministry matters they discussed. God had Brian's replacement waiting. Paul de Jong grew up in the Lower Hutt church in New Zealand. He trained in Faith Bible College. After doing evangelistic work he found his way on to our staff in Sydney. Surely God knew the future when He brought Paul to us. His business skills lay dormant until a new church was required.

Once more Frank began to 'see' a place where young people, in fact people of any age, could develop their gifts and ministries for God.

'Brian, I feel God would have us establish a college which will combine theology with the arts,' Frank said to his son one night. Brian immediately caught the vision.

'A great idea dad.' How alike these two are, I thought as I listened. They think alike. They minister alike. Amazing. They tossed ideas back and forth until a pattern began to emerge. The difficulty would be finding someone capable of heading up such a college. The person would need to have the same vision and high qualifications.

The standard must be one of excellence. It was when Brian visited America that he found the man he believed would be just right. He phoned his father.

'Dad, I think I have found your man for the college. You remember David Johnston who came to Australia with The Red Letter Edition group?'

'Yes.'

'I've been telling him about your vision for a college. Would you believe he has the same dream.'

As far as any of us knew no such college existed anywhere in the world.

'Sound him out to see if he would be interested.'

Yes, David and Marianna Johnston would be prepared to come. Within a few months the International Institute for Creative Ministries was birthed round our dining room table as curriculum and staffing were discussed. All this would stretch the budget to the limit. Yet if the vision was really from God miracles would happen.

It seemed that God was stretching the church again when we were once more forced out of our building. There had always been opposition from the owners, who appeared to hate Christians. Now they had been offered a higher rental and we had to pay that or quit. We chose to quit.

'Why put money in the pockets of the heathen?' Frank asked. This time we would buy our own building.

That was when he discovered the scarcity of buildings with parking facilities the size we needed. It must be in an area not too far from our present building. For two years we looked. In the meantime the church had to meet in six different auditoriums.

The fringe people fell off but the foundations were such that the main body of our people stayed with us, suffering the difficulties with the pastors. Ten years ago we'd thought the days of putting up and pulling down sound equipment every Sunday was a thing of the past. Here we were at it again. Few knew the commitment needed by the team who were out by six every Sunday morning moving gear into place.

What a blessing in a time when commitment seems to be a very scarce commodity. We thrilled at the giving of our people. Strikes, on-site payments demanded by the unions and extra demands by the city council even after they had passed the plans made the cost blow way out beyond the budget. Can we be anything but thankful for faithfulness in giving by God's people when many Christian projects outside the church thrust their claims ahead of the home base. Most of our people practised the principles of tithing. They also gave sacrificially to the new building.

The whole project became a repeat of the beginning days in the old building in Goulburn Street. Builders working during the week. Services in one section on Sundays. Often men were waiting to start work the moment the meeting ended. Three months later than we had planned we dedicated the facility to God. Our staff, now seven full-time and two lay pastors, grew into a loyal team. Frank has always sought to pour into his staff lessons learned by his experience.

Some of these men are already planning to expand into other essential ministries. Exit ministries to homosexuals. Loving care ministries to the needy. The challenge of teen suicide, stated to be the highest killer of young people. There are also thieves around as we discovered when a volunteer worker's handbag went missing. The war against evil never ends. But God has given the church all the tools needed to accomplish the task and Frank has used every one of them in the ministry.

Chapter 14

THE THIEF IS SITTING IN CHURCH

'Hazel, the man at the garage is having a heart attack,' Frank suddenly called out one afternoon when he was taking a rest – which meant praying and speaking in tongues.

'I didn't hear the telephone ring,' I replied.

'It didn't,' Frank said.

'Then how could you know that?' I asked in wonder. Frank thought it more profitable to ask the Lord than to discuss it with me. He went back to praying.

'Lord, why are you showing me this?' In answer he received a deep impression that God would show him for His glory things out of the past, in the present and the future which he could not know naturally. Two days later we drove into the service station to buy petrol. A stranger served us.

'Where's Jim?' Frank asked.

'He had a heart attack a couple of days ago and ended up in hospital.' So what Frank had seen was right.

Ray Bloomfield's teaching on the gifts of the Holy Spirit created Frank's hunger for them to operate in his own ministry, but when he was still a Salvation Army officer he'd read *Echoes And Memories* written by Bramwell Booth, the Army's second General. The book tells of the supernatural acts of God in the early-day meetings of the Salvation Army.

These ranged from levitations through to the gift of tongues to healing by the power of God and 'prostrations'. William Booth himself had written about the value of the gifts in an article printed in a *War Cry* dated 1914.

'There is not a word in the Bible which proves we may not have them (spiritual gifts) at the present time and there is nothing in experience to show they would not be as useful today as in any period of the church's history,' he wrote. 'Far be it for me to say one word that would stay the longing of any heart for the extraordinary gifts mentioned... I believe in their necessity... By all means let us have the perfection of the divine method of working. Then this infidel world should be made to see all of God that is possible, in order that it may believe.'

'That's what I want,' Frank declared. 'Lord, grant your servant the ability to use the gifts as you intended them to be used.' God answered with the unexpected image of the man who sold us our petrol. Frank describes the word of knowledge this way: 'I see a picture in my mind. Sometimes it's like seeing the face of someone you know very well. Other times it's simply a deep sense of knowing something.'

Fearful at first that he could be wrong when he was giving a word of knowledge he was somewhat hindered. Then he determined he would trust God and let his fears go. 'My first impression has always been the right one,' he says. Sometimes the revelation has been startling.

Like the time he saw the thief sitting in church. There had been thefts of sound equipment, musical instruments, expensive Bibles from the book-shop and wallets from the offices. The thieves were so quick and shrewd that we had not been able to catch them.

Frank was taking a group to Seoul, Korea, for a church growth seminar when he received a telex in Hong Kong saying the church had again been robbed of its electrical equipment. As Frank prayed on

Sunday morning, before the group joined him for a communion service, he put a question to the Lord.

'Lord, who is it robbing the church? Show me so that I can deal with the problem.' Frank saw clearly in his mind a young blond-haired man sitting in the auditorium.

'Lord, why are you showing me this?' Frank asked again.

Clearly the Lord made him know that this was the young man masterminding and committing the robberies. Frank decided to share what he had seen with his travelling companions when they met in his room.

'I want you to know God has shown me by a word of knowledge who robs the church.' He described what he had seen. That night Frank phoned through to the church service in Sydney as he usually did when on an overseas trip. Brian was leading.

'Dad, we have a new chorus we want to sing to you,' he said when the call came through.

'Not now Brian. I have a word of knowledge for the church. God has shown me who is stealing our equipment.' The people fell silent and the atmosphere was charged with tension. 'Brian, he is a young man with blond, shoulder-length hair sitting at the back of the auditorium on your right.'

Every blond-headed man, no matter where he was sitting, fell under the gaze of the congregation. One in particular gradually slipped lower in his seat.

'If that young man will stay behind after the service Brian will help him to find peace with God,' Frank continued. No one stayed. A few weeks later the safes went missing on a holiday weekend. Sue, Frank's secretary, decided to work on the Monday although it was a public holiday. She discovered a gaping hole in the front door with a million pieces of glass spread across the carpet. Frank grumbled as he answered the telephone. Didn't everybody know this was a public holiday and we were going for a picnic.

It was Sue. 'Pastor, someone's broken into the church. They've been in the offices and the print shop but I don't think anything is missing.'

'What about the safes?' Frank asked.

'I didn't think of that. I'll check for you.' In a moment she was back with the information that the safes had gone.

'Phone the police and don't touch anything. I'll be right in.'

'I've already phoned them and they are coming to look for fingerprints.'

'How could anyone have moved those two safes? The old one was so heavy and they were bolted together,' I said as we drove into town. 'Do you think they knew there had been a missions offering as well as the ordinary offering last night?'

'Probably. There would have been $12,000 in those safes,' Frank said.

'Plus the bookshop money,' I added.

We sat forlornly staring at the broken glass while we waited for the police. Who could have done this? It was awful to think that someone from the congregation would stoop to taking what belonged to God. While we were still thinking about it a young man we affectionately called 'Mitch' appeared at the door.

'Mitch' had roughed it in life until he'd become a Christian.

'Don't touch anything. There's been a robbery,' Frank told him.

'I know. That's what I've come to see you about.'

'Then you had better come into my office.' As the two of them walked through the office door my heart felt numb. Although Mitch was backsliding surely he didn't do it.

I remembered how he had taught himself to read from the Living Bible. 'Please Lord, don't let it be Mitch.'

It wasn't Mitch but he knew the culprits. As the story unfolded we again wondered at the ways of God.

'I went to the pub with my two flatmates to have some drinks. While we drank they unfolded their plan to break into the church and wanted me to join them.' He lowered his eyes during the telling of the story but raised them again as he told how he had refused to be part of the plot. These were two dangerous men with a list of convictions including armed robbery. Fear drove Mitch to go along with the plan but he prayed that somehow God would get him out of the situation.

They headed for a park to wait until the early hours of the morning when they were less likely to be discovered. Here they were attacked by a gang of youths. Mitch was knocked unconscious and ended up in hospital. The other two took the safes, blew them open, and escaped with the money over the border into the State of Victoria. One was the blond-haired boy of the word of knowledge. Three months elapsed without trace of the thieves.

Frank answered a long distance telephone call one day to find the caller was one of the thieves.

'Pastor Houston, I need your help. I'm one of the men who stole the church safes, I feel all churned up about it.

'What can I do? If I own up I'll go back to jail and I can't bear to think of that after all the years I've spent there.'

'You know Ralph, you have only one answer. That is to come back and face it. You will have no peace until you do. You didn't rob me or the church. That was God's money.' The phone clicked off. A week later Ralph made another phone call. He was back in town.

'Pastor, I'm coming round to see you but you must not phone the police until I tell you to.'

'I will be waiting,' Frank assured him. As time passed without sight of him Frank wondered if he was running so scared that he'd changed his mind. He'd know that with the police record his confession could mean a lengthy jail sentence. Perhaps nine years. But he did come, Bible under his arm and his face shining. 'Pastor, this thing is haunting me. I've been seeking God all night and I believe I have found him.' Frank made him a cup of coffee. For an hour they talked.

Ralph made a full confession of all the evil things he'd done.

'You can ring the head of the break-in squad now. I'm ready to give myself up.' The police reaction surprised Frank.

'Reverend, you shouldn't be alone with that man. He's dangerous. We'll be there in three minutes.'

They found Ralph drinking a second cup of coffee and talking quietly to Frank. He made a full confession of the crime against the church and a few others they knew nothing about.

'Ralph, we will have to take you in,' they said almost apologetically.

'I know. I'm ready,' Ralph told them as he stood up.

As they walked out to the waiting police car Frank wondered about the blond- haired fellow. Ten days after Ralph's arrest he turned up, confessing to another pastor that he was the instigator of the robbery. Had he listened when God spoke through the word of knowledge that Sunday night he could have saved himself and his friend nine months in jail. This was only one of many times when God worked supernaturally through the word of knowledge. Sometimes the gift has been startling in its detail as God has revealed things Frank could not possibly know any other way. This leaves no doubt who God wants to bless.

'There's a woman here tonight with a particular problem. I know what it is but I cannot tell you over the microphone,' Frank said in a camp meeting.

'God has shown me that you have in your purse a half-eaten roll of lifesavers, an opened letter from your daughter in Melbourne, a white handkerchief and a ten dollar note. If you come to me after the meeting I will tell you what to do about your problem.'

With the word of knowledge God had given a word of wisdom. One woman, with those specific items in her purse and no others, came to Frank for counsel. Some have strange ideas about words of knowledge. One woman complained that no one from the church had visited her husband when he was in hospital.

'Did you tell anyone he was in the hospital?' Frank asked.

'No. I expected you would have had a word of knowledge about it.'

'Really. Then you were wrong. God doesn't do what you can do yourself.'

Prophecy is misused as well when it becomes directional. Over the years there has always been someone ready to say that the Lord has shown them that Frank should go to a certain place or perform a certain task.

'That's strange. I was talking to God this morning and he didn't tell me. I wonder why he should tell you,' he replies. It was through prophecy that we lost a family to our church. When they visited another church the pastor prophesied over them.

'In all the time we attended Christian Life Centre we didn't have one prophecy. They really don't move in the Spirit.' Why disillusion them by telling them that particular church prophesies to anyone who attends for the first time. 'Prophesying them in' they call it.

'That isn't what prophecy is for, is it?' I asked Frank.

'Well it really isn't our concern,' he told me. He was non-committal as usual, refusing to criticise a brother. Tongues are frowned on by the critics of Pentecostal churches yet it was through a message in tongues that my sister and brother-in-law found Jesus. It was Ted's first visit to our church. Frank was out of town and I was nervous in case there was some manifestation of the Holy Spirit which would upset him. I was about to breathe freely as the meeting neared its end. Suddenly a young woman burst forth in a tongues message which was interpreted by an older man.

'Why did those two have to do this tonight?' I groaned within myself. 'Ted will be put off forever.' Frank never entertained such fears. He figured God knew what He was about. As soon as Ted arrived home he told my sister, Joyce, about the strange language he had heard in 'Frank's church'.

Joyce searched for a Bible hidden on top of a wardrobe, blew the dust off it and let it fall open. It happened to open at Acts 2:4. She read, 'and [they] began to speak with other tongues as the Spirit gave them utterance.' 'That's it. That's what they were doing,' Joyce cried excitedly.

'I must tell Ted.' For the first time since their marriage they decided to go to church for reasons other than business. Doesn't the Bible say in 1 Corinthians 14:22 that tongues were a sign to the unbeliever? That experience helped me to agree with Frank.

We needn't worry for God does know best. They were also a sign at a wedding when Frank spoke in tongues and with the interpretation during the service. At the reception the bridegroom's father asked Frank where he had learned the Basque language.

'I haven't learned the Basque language,' Frank assured him.

'But you spoke perfect Basque in the service and translated it into perfect English.'

'That was God speaking through one of the gifts He has given to the church. God is still speaking to men today if they will only listen,' Frank explained. Here was an opportunity to tell the man about God.

'Such experiences could only be the Spirit of God using an earthly vessel,' Frank explained as wedding guests also asked questions about the phenomena. Other events have proved the gifts as relevant today as when Paul recorded them.

'In the realm of spirits some supernatural gift is needed to help people,' Frank explained when I questioned him about deliverance.

'Remember the old man who sat at the back of the church in Lower Hutt? When I asked him had he ever committed his life to Christ he told me he wanted to but something always stopped him.'

'I remember. God showed you he had a spirit of unbelief controlling his actions. After you ordered the spirit to leave in the name of Jesus the old man told you he could give his life to Jesus then and he did.'

Occasionally someone has given all the appearance of being a committed Christian with the Holy Spirit in control yet they behaved in a questionable way. What Christian would interrupt an altar call with religious jargon when the preacher was praying for people. But one woman did. Frank perceived a religious spirit which was certainly not the Holy Spirit. Once freed in the name of Jesus she sat quietly through the rest of the service.

'How can you know which spirit operates in a person's life?' I asked him.

'It's the same inner awareness as I have with the other gifts. The Holy Spirit makes me to know what spirit is operating; whether it is man's spirit, an evil spirit or the Holy Spirit.

'Discerning of spirits the Bible calls it in 1 Corinthians 12,' he told me.

In some other cultures Frank finds 'demon possession' common. In a letter he sent from Sri Lanka he told of a beautifully dressed young woman who sat on the front seat in every meeting of the crusade.

'One night when I was preaching she began to make strange body movements.

'I didn't want any interruption so I bound the spirit in the name Jesus,' he wrote. 'She came on the altar call. When I mentioned the name of Jesus she screamed and her neck swelled like a balloon. She leaned over backwards so far her head literally touched the floor.

'This had to be something supernatural. I began to name the demons. Strange names I had not heard before. The local pastor told me they were the names of gods which abound in Sri Lanka. When I had cast out the last one the girl became normal,' the letter concluded. Frank prayed that the Holy Spirit would occupy the place of demon spirits so that there was no room for them to return as long as she did not open her life to them again by neglecting her relationship with God.

It cannot be said that the ministry is dull. Frank was reaching an important point in his message when a man began to utter such blasphemies that the ladies and visitors in the church were embarrassed. 'Deacons, please take this man out and minister to him,' Frank ordered. The man fought all the way down the aisle. Turning to the congregation Frank explained that the man was obviously demon possessed.

'I will have to teach the demons to cast out the deacons,' he announced with all solemnity. The congregation exploded into laughter.

'Don't you mean teach the deacons to cast out demons?' his assistant pastor asked.

'Of course.' Frank was never one to admit to embarrassment.

'Well it broke the tension,' he told me later.

Nor was there any embarrassment the night he rushed into the hospital ward to pray for Audrey Penny. She and her husband, Des, were Australians ministering in evangelism in New Zealand. Des was in Adelaide, South Australia, for a series of meetings when Audrey was taken seriously ill. Their fourteen-year-old son phoned.

'Pastor Houston, Mum is sick. Will you come and pray for her.' We discovered that Audrey had collapsed but refused to go to hospital. We could see she was desperately ill.

'Audrey, you can't stay here. We'll arrange for some of our people to care for the four older children and you and the two little ones can stay with us. She told us she was haemorrhaging but still she wouldn't see a doctor. By the next morning I knew she was at danger point. Frank had gone out by the time she collapsed. I yelled at the two elders who were working in our yard.

'Go in and pray for Audrey while I phone the doctor. She needs help urgently.' The doctor called the ambulance – I was relieved when she was in expert care. The shrill tones of the telephone woke us at 2 am the next morning.

'This is the hospital. Are you Mrs Penny's next of kin?'

'We have accepted responsibility for her in her husband's absence.'

'Then you had better come straight away. She is in a critical condition.' Frank threw on his clothes telling me to phone our praying people as he did so. 'Get all who can to come to the church straight away for prayer.' Once I'd done that I prayed as well.

At the hospital Frank charged straight up to Audrey's bed, ignoring the doctor and nurses working frantically to save her life. Frank felt a burst of faith as he placed his hands on her head, commanding 'life to replace death in this woman'. Audrey opened her eyes and smiled wanly. As he walked out the door of the ward with the sister she told him that when she phoned us they had been unable to get any pulse or blood pressure.

Frank joined the others in the church. Two hours later the burden was replaced by a sense of incredible peace and assurance that we had received our answer. Audrey would recover. That was why it was a shock when the hospital rang next morning to say that Audrey must undergo surgery.

'We don't know if she is strong enough to stand it,' the nurse said. Fear leapt into my heart. Frank had gone to church and I was alone. I would not accept this. God had given us all the assurance Audrey would live. Faith triumphed. Audrey did live. We thanked God for His gift of extraordinary faith. The gifts are tools to be used for the benefit of the human race, not toys to be played with at the whim of the carnal Christian.

'Do you think carnality has been a reason for the gifts dying in the church? Haven't pastors been afraid that someone might abuse the gifts by using them for their own ends?' I really wanted to know.

'Maybe, but we should not be afraid to handle such situations,' Frank replied. Come to think of it, I have heard Frank tell the congregation that a tongues message a person gave was from their own spirit and not for everybody. I have also heard him say following an interpretation, 'Now here is the correct interpretation.' Afterwards he will take the person aside to explain where he believed they were wrong.

This gives a congregation a sense of security. Because spiritual gifts have been one factor which have contributed to the fruitfulness of Frank's ministry he desires to teach his own young men to move in that realm.

'Don't be afraid to use the gifts,' he tells them. 'There are many factors which contribute to church growth. In the Acts of the Apostles growth was frequently due to the fact that the miraculous caught the attention of vast numbers of people. This in turn gave them an open ear to hear the gospel, to which they responded.

'Let us believe God to see the miraculous in our meetings that we may catch the attention of the masses.' If Frank has any fear, it is that the church will again lose the use of these valuable God-given tools.

196

Chapter 15

REFIRING

On a Friday in late September, 1985, Frank and I arrived home from a church growth seminar at the Yoido Full Gospel Church in Seoul, Korea. On Sunday Frank knew he was in trouble. At 8.15 am he parked the car and started up the stairs to the auditorium. He puzzled over the difficulty he had in putting one foot in front of the other. I'd walked on ahead not realising that Frank was ill. There had been some symptoms in Seoul but we had not realised their portent. Ten minutes into his sermon he felt as though he was going to faint. To avoid that embarrassment he sat on the edge of the platform.

'I'm feeling ill. Will the elders lay hands on me.' The elders were at his side in a flash. 'Lord, heal your servant from the top of his head to the soles of his feet,' one shouted. 'Devil, get your hands off God's servant,' ordered another. A doctor in the congregation followed Frank out to his office.

'Do you have any pain?' he asked.

'No. Just an unbelievable weakness.' I chipped in with the details of Frank's experience in Seoul and Gordon knew the problem. After a brief examination he gave his verdict. 'Frank, I think you have a duodenal ulcer and you are haemorrhaging. You've lost all your colour.

I want to take you for a blood test.'

'No Gordon, not now. I'm going to preach in the second service.' Gordon realised that here was a difficult patient who would follow the plan he had mapped out for his day no matter what anyone said. Well, he would pray for his pastor. God did heal the sick apart from medicine.

'I'll send someone to the house tomorrow to get a blood sample. In the meantime let me know if you get any worse.' By Monday Frank nearly fell on the floor when he climbed out of bed. Once the blood sample was taken we waited impatiently for the results. Early afternoon Gordon rang.

'Frank your haemoglobin level is down to seven point nine. It should be about fifteen. You must get to the hospital immediately.'

'What does that mean?' Frank wanted to know.

'It means you are seriously ill and you must not delay getting treatment. You will need blood transfusions.' 'Well Gordon, I am not going to the hospital until the elders of the church have anointed me with oil. The Bible doesn't say call the doctor. It says call the elders and that I am going to do.'

'How long will that take?' The doctor sounded anxious.

'About an hour.'

'You don't have an hour.'

'Gordon, I am not going to the hospital till I've called the elders.'

'Then go immediately the elders have prayed for you. I'll phone the hospital to let them know you are coming.' While Frank waited for the elders our daughter, Maureen, read some of his favourite Scriptures. When the elders anointed Frank with oil nothing seemed to happen physically but he was filled with an incredible peace and sense of well-being. At five o'clock we helped Frank through the hospital door. A nurse whipped the colourless man into a wheelchair before he sank to the ground.

'This is humiliation indeed. I hope none of my congregation see me now,' he said to me. 'This man of faith and power now weak and unable to walk.' But one did – the nurse in charge of the ward. All day he had wondered why he was in 'admission'. He'd never worked there before. As he walked beside Frank into the ward he was sure that God had placed him there to minister to his pastor. While the nursing staff rushed to work taking blood tests and asking endless questions they searched for veins in which they could insert a drip. They had difficulty finding one.

Frank, lying relaxed in a bubble of peace, detached himself from the turmoil, centring his mind on the Lord. By now his haemoglobin level was down to four. Anxiety pushed to take control of my mind. The doctor had said he would need blood transfusions.

Blood transfusions – their safety still uncertain although the doctor had exploded when Frank asked the risk.

'I'm sick and tired of AIDS.' That's all right for her Frank thought. She isn't getting the blood. I thought of the possibility of a haemorrhage but that Frank could die didn't occur to me. I went home to bed. As I sank into its comfort I relinquished the whole situation to Jesus.

'Lord, I can do nothing for Frank except pray. I place him and myself in your everlasting arms.' At that moment of surrender God's amazing peace also surrounded me and I slept unaware of the drama at the hospital. At one o'clock in the morning Frank's blood pressure dropped alarmingly. Doctors worked frantically.

'We are sorry Mr Houston but we are having trouble with your blood pressure.' Frank removed his oxygen mask briefly.

'Just keep working on it doctor.' Frank slipped the mask back over his nose. 'At this moment of serious trouble I sensed the weakness of my body yet I was amazingly strong in spirit until I lay in a beautiful stillness,' he told me later.

'I committed myself totally to God's will. I had never been aware of the Holy Spirit in this way. Jesus was very near and precious. I saw the work He had been doing in me all through the years,' he told me.

'All the trials, temptations and difficulties were paying off. What I had preached from the Word of God was the truth. I also knew how fragile life is but if dying is like this I'll never be afraid to die.'

As Frank recounted his experiences I saw that he had made the same discovery as I had when I read Psalm 66:8–12. God had brought us into a wealthy place. Yet in some notes Frank made about his illness he wrote, 'Lord give me a few more years that I might go out of this life having achieved something for God.'

I wondered about that prayer. Hadn't he achieved about all he could in forty-three years of ministry. Why else did he receive an honorary doctorate for his work in Bible colleges and a grandfather clock from the Assemblies of God churches of the State of New South Wales when he had completed forty years of ministry. Why did our son, Brian, pay us the greatest tribute that a son could pay his parents? I realised that Frank was reassessing the ministry.

I concluded it wasn't what he had done that counted but what still remained to be done. This challenge made him wonder why there are so many 'Once-a-Sunday Christians'. He remembers that Sunday was totally given over to God when he was a young Christian. No time for picnics or football or cleaning shoes.

Perhaps we were too restrictive on Sunday activities then but have we swung to the other extreme now? Frank still insists we are engaged in warfare and we must be committed to winning it. For this reason he will not be diverted from preaching the pure gospel with integrity.

He speaks with concern when he says, 'We are dealing with people's lives and God will hold us accountable for the results. It is important to me to be able to walk into my pulpit knowing I am a man of God, able to speak the oracles of God. To meet the hurts – the sin of other human beings.'

If it was not so what might have happened to the homosexual who phoned for help from three thousand miles. He was a bright, active Christian in our church until a scholarship took him to Los Angeles to pursue his career in television.

There he became actively involved in homosexuality and we lost contact with him. After three years his brother phoned to say he was home in Perth, dying with cancer. At this time our morning service was televised and sent nationwide by the Australian Broadcasting Corporation. A friend of the Smiths phoned to tell them to watch the service. Mrs Smith flicked through the channels to One.

'Mum, that's Pastor Houston's church in Sydney. I want to talk to him.' We'd only been home half an hour when the phone rang. 'This is Mrs Smith from Perth. Jim watched your service on Channel One. He's very ill and extremely weak but he wants to talk to you.'

She passed the phone to Jim. 'Pastor Houston, can you help me? I'm dying with AIDS. The doctor says I only have two weeks left and I know I'll go to hell.' Jim was extremely distressed.

'I've committed the most awful sins and I'm sure God can't forgive me.' His loud crying almost prevented him from speaking.

'Listen Jim, God does love you no matter what you have done.' Frank felt his pain. This young man, so full of promise – dying – and with AIDS.

'I can't believe that. I deliberately turned away from God. How can he forgive that?'

'Jim, God does love you. He hates your sin but he does love you. He asks you to tell Him that you have sinned and when you ask for His forgiveness I know He will forgive.' Jim stumbled through a prayer of confession and a plea for the Lord to take away his guilt. The phone clicked off. Two weeks later Jim died. Frank was stirred in his spirit. Life must go on. The living still cried for help. Who but the church has the real answers to life.

'I am more important to my city than the Lord Mayor is,' Frank tells his congregation. 'And so are you. When we forget the church is about God and people, not money or buildings or "fad" doctrines, we run into trouble.' He is adamant that he doesn't want to know how many are in church. Only how many are outside waiting to be brought in.

'Let us hold fast the course God has set us. Stay with the simple gospel of salvation, healing and the baptism of the Holy Spirit. That is all a man needs.

'We are created by God and for God and until people come to know him they haven't found the answer to life.'

I heard Brian and Frank discussing the health of the church. 'The ministry will only stay alive as long as men will allow God to work through them,' Frank said. For this reason he implants into younger men the vision and dreams of the ministry as he sees them. 'Blessed are the pure in heart for they shall see.' Frank stopped reading the Beatitude right there. The pure in heart are visionaries. They see the unfolding revelation of the will of God. As Frank mulled over the words he knew he had another sermon.

'The things you taught us have been a big help in my Christian life,' wrote Chris Aiton, now a successful missionary in the Philippines. Frank encourages them to see and hear from God themselves.

'Then you cannot lose for winning.' Frank made a resolution he will not break when he said, as he closed the pages of *Smith Wigglesworth – Apostle of Faith*, 'I will not listen to negative men nor read negative books.' Frank believes negativity is a killer and men who get into that realm will hinder the life and work of the church.

He threw out another challenge to the ministers at the 1988 New South Wales Assemblies of God conference when he said, 'God can take a worm like me and a worm like you, for I'm not the only worm, and empower us to turn the world around us upside down. God hasn't changed. Let us say, "To hell with the devil" then get on with the job God has given his people.'

At sixty-six Frank states positively, 'I'm not going to retire, I'm going to refire.'

Isn't that what life's all about?

Other Marshall Pickering Paperbacks

ISSUES FACING CHRISTIANS TODAY

John Stott

In this major appraisal of contemporary social and moral questions, John Stott defines Christian thought on the complex global, social and sexual issues that confront us and provides a valuable resource for Christians responding to the need to seek the renewal of society. £5.95

Issues Facing Christians Today – Study Guide compiled by Lance Pierson. £1.50

THE SACRED DIARY OF ADRIAN PLASS AGED 37¾
Illustrated by Dan Donovan

Adrian Plass

A full-length, slide-splitting paperback based on the hilarious diary entries in Christian Family magazine of Adrian Plass, 'an amiable but somewhat inept Christian'. By his own confession, Adrian 'makes many mistakes and is easily confused', but a reasssuring sense of belonging to the family of God is the solid, underlying theme. Best-selling Christian book of 1987. £2.50

THE THEATRICAL TAPES OF LEONARD THYNN

Adrian Plass

The final volume of Adrian Plass's Christian trilogy. All the familiar characters from the Sacred Diary of Adrian Plass and The Horizontal Epistles of Andromeda Veal are taking part in recording sessions to produce Leonard Thynn's extraordinary theatrical tapes. They produce a dramatic version of 'Daniel in the Lion's Den' which of course you will never be able to read in the same way again. £2.99

THE HORIZONTAL EPISTLES OF ANDROMEDA VEAL
Illustrated by Dan Donovan

Adrian Plass

Adrian Plass – diary-writer *sans pareil* – returns! This time he finds much to amuse him in the letters of Andromeda Veal, precocious eleven-year-old daughter of a Greenham woman. During a stay in hospital, Andromeda reveals herself as a shrewd commentator on her local church and the wider world, and seizes her chance to write all those letters that had to wait before – to, 'Gorgeous Chops', 'Ray Gun', 'Rabbit' Runcie, the Pope, and even Cliff Richard. £2.50

THE CROSS AND THE SWITCHBLADE

David Wilkerson

One of the best sellers of Christian paperbacks! An amazing and breathtaking description of one man's adventure in faith into New York gangland. If Christianity can work here it will work anywhere.

No Christian should miss this modern Acts of the Apostles. £1.95

JONI

Joni Eareckson Tada

In this international bestseller, Joni, the victim of an accident that left her totally paralysed from the neck down, reveals the struggle to accept and adjust to her handicap.

Joni's story has been made into a full length feature film. £1.95

THE TORN VEIL

Gulshan Esther, with Thelma Sangster

Gulshan Fatima, the youngest daughter of a Muslim Sayed family, lived a quietly secluded life at home in the Punjab. A trip to England began a spiritual awakening that led ultimately to her conversion to Christianity. She has since preached to thousands of Muslims and many not only have found faith but have, like her, found physical healing. £1.95